Troublemaking

Lydia Hughes is a workplace organiser. She was the Head of Organising at the IWGB until 2021. She has been involved in organising with foster care workers, food delivery couriers, cycling instructors, cleaners, security guards, and game workers. She now supports socialist education initiatives and is active as a union member. She is an Editor at *Notes from Below* and *Red Pepper*.

Jamie Woodcock works for a university and is a researcher based in London. He is a member of two unions, the IWGB and UCU. He supports new worker organising through the IWGB General Members branch and the Organise Now project. Jamie is an editor at *Notes from Below* and *Historical Materialism* and the author of *Working the Phones* and *Marx at the Arcade*.

Troublemaking

Why You Should Organize Your Workplace

LYDIA HUGHES
JAMIE WOODCOCK

VERSO

London • New York

First published by Verso 2023

1 3 5 7 9 10 8 6 4 2

Verso
UK: 6 Meard Street, London W1F 0EG
US: 388 Atlantic Avenue, Brooklyn, NY 11217
versobooks.com

Verso is the imprint of New Left Books

ISBN-13: 978-1-83976-710-4
ISBN-13: 978-1-83976-711-1 (UK EBK)
ISBN-13: 978-1-83976-714-2 (US EBK)

British Library Cataloguing in Publication Data
A catalogue record for this book is available from the British Library

Library of Congress Cataloging-in-Publication Data
A catalog record for this book is available from the Library of Congress

Typeset in Monotype Fournier by Hewer Text UK Ltd, Edinburgh
Printed and bound by CPI Group (UK) Ltd, Croydon, CR0 4YY

To all the troublemakers, past, present and future.

In 50 years' time, who will they remember? They will remember Rosa Parks. They will remember Martin Luther King. You should be a troublemaker. Be a troublemaker, make a difference. Don't go through life, looking at things that are bad and do nothing about it. So have courage and step up. And there will be consequences to that. Sometimes you'll be there on your own. But often enough people will recognize that kind of organic leadership, that leadership which stays close to its base, that doesn't climb the greasy pole, doesn't look to have an easier life as a full time official. You have to work overtime, you have to get up and do the night shift, you have to suffer the boss's tongue and discipline. The closer you are to that, then at the time of the explosion, you'll be in the right position. So it's really important to be a troublemaker. Being a working class hero is something to be, actually, so you have to step forward. And if you've got youth on your side, then you've got 40 years of struggle ahead.

– Willie Black, Scottish trade unionist
and community activist for fifty-two years

CONTENTS

Acknowledgements

Both authors would like to thank the Verso team who made this book possible while fighting a union battle themselves. Particularly, we would like to thank Ben for the initial support with the idea, and Rosie for all the advice and guidance for making the book happen.

To all of our fellow organizers from what is always a difficult but joyful struggle, thank you: Henry, Alex, Jason, Charlie, Max, Catherine, Aidan, Maritza, Mateus, to name but a few. For reading the book and giving comments, thank you Austin, Ashley, Clarissa, Natalie, Ben, Dante, Matthew, Clark, Wendy, Sai, Callum, Laura, Chaz, Jake, Casper, Nancy, Hilary. For the debates and discussions that formed that book, thank you to our fellow *Notes from Below* editors.

Lydia would like to thank Jamie for his unfaltering love and patience that made this book possible. I hope our ability to have political debates over the dinner table makes this book all the more rich. To have a partner in life and in writing is rare and special. I especially want to thank my parents,

Vanessa and Phil, for their encouragement. Your company in the ceramic studio kept me sane. For your support and friendship through the process, thank you Bobby, Miranda, Natalie, Ben, Laetitia, Ellioté, Ciara, Casper, Nancy, Bebe, Charlie, Tessa, Sunny and Persis and so many more.

Jamie would like to thank Lydia for her continuing support and love throughout the book writing – and much more widely. We have organized together for a long time, but writing a book brings its own challenges, which you have addressed with both kindness and determination. Writing a book is never just the work of the authors and I would like to thank everyone who has contributed both directly and indirectly. In particular, thanks to my family and friends, as well as everyone else with whom I've had book-related conversations along the way.

GLOSSARY

ACAS – Advisory, Conciliation and Arbitration Service

ACFTU – All-China Federation of Trade Unions

ALU – Amazon Labor Union

ASOS – action short of strike

BA – British Airways

BMC – Brihanmumbai Municipal Corporation

CEO – chief executive officer

CGT – Confédération générale du travail (General Confederation of Labour)

CIPD – Chartered Institute of Personnel and Development

CNT – Confederación Nacional del Trabajo (National Confederation of Labour)

EETPU – Electrical, Electronic, Telecommunications and Plumbing Union

EPIU – Electricians, Plumbers Industrial Union

HMRC – Her Majesty's Revenue and Customs

HR – human resources

ISIL – Islamic State of Iraq and the Levant

IWGB – Independent Workers' Union of Great Britain

IWW – Industrial Workers of the World

KVSS – Kachra Vahatuk Shramik Sangh (Garbage Transport Workers' Union)

LSE – London School of Economics and Political Science

MPs – members of parliament

NHS – National Health Service

NIMBY – not in my backyard

NLRB – National Labor Relations Board (United States)

PKK – Partiya Karkerên Kurdistan (Kurdistan Workers' Party)

PSOE – Partido Socialista Obrero Español (Spanish Socialist Workers' Party)

PYD – Partiya Yekîtiya Demokrat (Kurdish Democratic Union Party)

RMT – National Union of Rail, Maritime and Transport Workers

SEIU – Service Employees International Union

TDL – The Doctors Laboratory

TGWU – Transport and General Workers' Union

TUC – Trades Union Congress

UCL – University College London

UCU – University and College Union

UGT – Unión General de Trabajadores (General Union of Workers)

UNSA – Union nationale des syndicats autonomes (National Union of Autonomous Trade Unions)

USS – Universities Superannuation Scheme

UVW – United Voices of the World

YPG – Yekîneyên Parastina Gel (People's Defense Units)

Introduction

When we think about our engagement with democracy, it is often limited to putting a cross in a box every four or five years. Beyond that, we might choose who to work for, but we have almost no control once in our workplaces. If we try to change things, we get labelled troublemakers.

There is a pervasive idea that the labour movement has fallen on hard times, and this is paired with a longing for the well-organized workplaces and strong trade unions of the past. However, there is no going back. Instead, we must learn from the labour movement's historical high points and build something even better. This, as we will argue throughout the book, starts by becoming a troublemaker and getting organized at work.

Those of us looking for a future beyond capitalism have reached a crossroad. Jeremy Corbyn and Bernie Sanders were a focus for many campaigning for a different kind of world. Socialist ideas seemed to finally be coming back into the mainstream. A survey in 2021 found that 67 per cent of young people in Britain wanted a 'socialist economic system'. Respondents blamed capitalism for climate change and the housing crisis, and they wanted to defend the NHS and nationalize key industries.[1] Similar studies in the US have shown the majority of young people have a positive view of socialism.[2]

Now, the Corbyn experiment has collapsed, and Bernie's chances at getting elected president seem as far away as ever. For many of us, change feels out of reach. In the US, the Black Lives Matter movement erupted in 2020 into the biggest uprising in US history. While some of that energy has gone into further organizing, a lot of it has dissipated. We cannot let all the struggle and politicization of the last few years go to waste. It is urgent that we collectively find a way forward.

We are not short of opportunities for troublemaking. The daily onslaught from our bosses and governments brings many chances to organize. It is up to us to recognize them and, most importantly, to take action. We start from the simple proposition that ordinary people have the power to change the world, and this book asserts that workplace struggles are a key part of how we can do so. If we want to build a radical alternative to capitalism, we need to start at its everyday foundations.

In the workplace we face capitalism's contradictions, but we also have the power to fight them. That is why we should wear the label of 'troublemaker' with pride. We may consider starting to develop our troublemaking power there by taking action over issues that seem small. For example, fixing the microwave in the break room or changing shifts around. Then we can build into something much more. However, if we cannot change our own work environments, how can we imagine changing the world? It is through these workplace struggles that we can develop the skills and confidence needed to make another kind of existence.

We have seen many moments where workers have become troublemakers. One started at the crack of dawn on a cold winter morning in 2019. We could see our breath as we made our way for the early shift on the picket lines at University College London (UCL). Striking cleaners and security guards were gathered outside the entrance to the university, refusing to work and picketing outside until the university met their demands. London's dull grey was pierced by the red flags hanging from the railings, along with handmade placards in bright colours. One simply stated 'SICK PAY NOW' in orange letters that matched the whistle being blown by the holder. Around a table with steaming hot cups of coffee, wrapped in scarves, workers demanded an end to outsourcing. They wanted UCL to bring their jobs back in-house. Spirits were high, helped by the crowd of supporters handing out coffee and leaflets from the stall.

The streets, which would usually be quiet at this time, were buzzing with activity. There was debate and discussion on the picket line. Even though the sun was not up yet, we felt the energy and excitement. A portable speaker blasted out reggaeton and some of the strikers were dancing.

Supporters brought breakfast and a few workers from other sites joined the picket on their way to work. A manager appeared, complaining about the blockage at the entrance, as if that was not the point of the picket line. A delivery driver asked what was happening. One of the workers explained why they were striking, how they were treated worse than when they worked in-house. The driver hopped back in the truck and headed off to another delivery, refusing to deliver there that day. This infuriated the manager, who marched back inside.

By 9 am, the crowd had grown. It included members from other branches of the Independent Workers' Union of Great Britain (IWGB), students, supporters and some academics. As the protest atmosphere built, someone on the megaphone suggested we march around the university. Red flares were lit, filling the entrance way with smoke, and the crowd headed off. The manager reappeared, looking worried and way out of his depth. The march caused a good amount of chaos on the campus, with red union flags and a banner that read: 'UCL END OUTSOURCING'. Maritza, who led the union branch, proudly held the middle of the banner. She had moved to London from Ecuador to work as a cleaner, then she had organized her workplace and become a leader in the union. She smiled as she talked to other workers.

The march stopped for speeches. We heard from a cleaner who said she was no longer afraid. She said the picketers deserve to be on the same conditions as other workers. A striking security guard took the microphone and called for support for the strike. He explained how he was treated differently than his co-workers, not having the same pay or holidays. Henry, the general secretary of the union, talked about his experience as a migrant worker at Senate House. He explained how they won an in-house campaign through strikes and protests like these. The speeches were translated back into Spanish, as many of the workers were from Latin America. Other speakers from the union shared their experiences of fighting elsewhere, while solidarity speeches from other unions expressed support. The strike carried on all day, with activities organized throughout. After finishing their shifts, many of the strikers headed to the pub to continue the debate over pints of Guinness.

UCL claimed on its website to be an 'accessible, publicly engaged organisation'.[3] Yet, it long denied these workers any say in the university. The university management relied on these workers to open, maintain and clean the buildings. Despite this, they outsourced them to a private company. The strike was a very public moment of confrontation with the deeply unequal nature of work at the university.

The following month, the workers struck again. This strike was coordinated with the University and College Union (UCU), which represents academic and some academic-related staff in British universities. Lecturers and professional staff began striking over a series of issues: pensions, pay, gender and ethnicity pay gaps, precarious contracts and workloads. The strike day brought workers from across campus. It was different from the previous strike, as both directly employed and outsourced workers joined the picket line. Strikers, students and supporters blocked entrances across the university. Workers across very different roles stood together, handing out leaflets and fighting collectively. At lunchtime a rally was called. We did a final tour of the picket lines before joining and were met with a surprise. There were so many people at the rally that the road outside the main entrance was blocked. When our group joined the rally we were met with clapping and cheering from the UCU members. Before the speeches started, red and blue flares were lit while workers chanted against UCL.

There were many smaller, not-so-public campaigns along the way, too – for example, over the use of surveillance technology. The outsourcing company tried to put in place a new time management system that involved biometric fingerprint scanners. The workers wrote a letter protesting this new discriminatory workplace monitoring. The company called a meeting to discuss the system, with managers trying to convince workers of the benefits. In response, workers disrupted the meeting, forcing the removal of the fingerprint machines. At UCL, workers have faced harassment, bullying, wage theft and more. The strikes were public battles in the campaign, but they were part of a much longer war.

Strikes can feel like the pinnacle of power at work. Yet the strike is always only the tip of the iceberg. Below the surface, before a strike, there has often been years of organizing and troublemaking. Much of the struggle between workers and management is hidden from public eyes.

It can feel insurmountable to change a large organization like UCL. The university has thousands of workers, layers of management and a budget of millions. Striking is such a powerful tool because it disrupts the workings of the organization. Changing the course of such a big institution can feel like moving a container ship, already set on a particular course. What can you do as one worker? Coming together to strike is like trying to stop huge engines. Without these motors, though, it does not matter what course the captain had planned. The captain fears icebergs, as they can lurk below the surface. But they also fear mutinies.

The strike is a powerful demonstration of the power of workers. Without workers, the university could not function. Managers and strike breakers needed to open the buildings, even if they had no idea where the keys were or how to disable the alarms. There were concerns about fire safety and what would happen if there was an accident. As a direct result of the strike, UCL management promised the outsourced workers the same terms and conditions as directly employed workers. This followed a campaign by workers at the neighbouring Senate House. After ten years of protests, strikes and a boycott, the workers were brought back in-house.

Work under capitalism – the thing that we will spend most of our lives doing – involves having to submit to the power of a boss and is thus, by its nature, not democratic. The rising popularity of socialist ideas has led to a surge of debate on how our lives and society are organized. Relationships at work, however, have remained relatively untouched by this radicalism, and so practicing these ideas at work might initially feel overwhelming. As Ursula Le Guin has explained: 'We live in capitalism, its power seems inescapable – but then, so did the divine right of kings. Any human power can be resisted and changed by human beings.'

If we want to overhaul society, the workplace is the setting in which to start. We are not arguing here that there is no role for political parties, voting, big demonstrations, occupations or other forms of political activity. But the key to a thorough-going revolution in how we live must come from wielding the power we have at work. This is where we come into the most direct conflict with capitalism and, without our work, it cannot function. We have the power to disrupt capitalism and we have the capability to build something else.

In the first part of this book, we introduce a range of different workplace struggles, particularly those of workers often deemed too precarious to organize: UK couriers' fight against precarious working conditions, despite a lack of employment status. Likewise, regardless of huge social barriers, waste collectors also found a way to fight back.

The flip side of this argument has also been used: that your conditions are too good for you to organize. We discuss the example of Kickstarter as part of the wider movement for organizing in the tech and games industries. Workers in these industries have shown what the fight for more control over work can look like today.

We then move on to discuss the huge victories of migrant cleaners organizing with UVW (United Voices of the World) to show how we can demand more at work than just pay and conditions – even though these are also important. The struggles of sans-papier workers in France show how wider demands can be brought into organizing. The next example, of the water wars in Bolivia, demonstrates how campaigns can fight for change way beyond the workplace. We survey examples of starting in the workplace, but fighting for liberation more widely. This means taking on questions around oppression, imperialism and solidarity.

In Part 2, we look at the concepts and ideas of work, particularly the dynamics, created by contradictory interests and pressure, that lead to workplace conflict. Worker organizing led historically to the formation of organisations like unions that have attempted to collectively bargain for improvements. As unions grow, they develop their own institutional interests, as well as a specialized layer of bureaucrats who are removed from the workplace. Unions are therefore subject to pressures from both employers and the rank-and-file membership, which can lead to unions playing a dual role under capitalism.

In Part 3, we argue for three principles to guide our organizing. First, we need action. In taking action we change the world, but this struggle also changes us. Action should furthermore be a core part of what we do rather than a last resort. Second, we need to find ways to build a rank and file that keeps union bureaucracy in check, developing methods and skills to apply pressure inside unions as well as the confidence to act for ourselves. Third, enacting democracy means understanding organizing as a process. We want to win, and this necessitates having as many co-workers involved in our struggle as possible. This might mean decisions not going our way or having to learn hard lessons. Struggle is not only about winning, it is also a process that builds new leaders and a confident rank and file. It is through struggle that we become a force capable of changing the world. We also introduce the idea of workers' inquiry. This builds upon the idea that we, as workers, are best placed to both understand and change our own work.

Fundamentally, our argument is this: you should become a troublemaker in your workplace. We often feel our most powerless as individuals at work, but by organizing collectively it can be where we are most powerful. Being a troublemaker is about finding ways to develop and wield our power, both to change our working conditions and to change the world beyond our workplace. We must fight for the climate, to end oppression and discrimination of all kinds and, of course, to build a new and better society in the process. In order to do this, we have to be willing to take action, build rank-and-file power and organize democratically.

Who we are

The ideas in this book are the culmination of years of conversations on picket lines, community centres and union offices, mainly in Britain, where we live. We have also been lucky to spend time talking to organizers in the US, India, Argentina, South Africa, Brazil and across Europe. We did not come up with these ideas in isolation; they come from experiences and comrades across the movement.

Lydia learned about politics through occupations, squats and at demonstrations. While she was a student, she had a chance encounter on Facebook with a cleaner campaign. She became involved in the cleaners' struggle at the London School of Economics (LSE). This was a formative experience, witnessing the building and wielding of real power at the workplace. It took her out of the collective depression of student politics, with A to B marches that seemed to have little impact on anything. From there she began working for the sister union of the LSE cleaners, the IWGB. The IWGB was established in 2012 by Latin American cleaners in London. They wanted a union that spoke their language, supported their community and addressed the unique challenges of outsourced cleaning work. The union has since grown to more than 6,000 members, recruiting migrant and precarious workers from other sectors. Lydia worked first with foster care workers and then with food delivery couriers, Uber drivers, cycling instructors, cleaners, security guards and game workers. Lydia was the IWGB's head of organizing until 2021. She remains active in recruiting co-workers in the shop where she works.

Jamie's involvement in organizing started as a teenage student during the invasion of Iraq. After his involvement in the Stop the War protests, he went on to university and was part of occupations in solidarity with Palestine, then took part in protests against austerity and student fees. During the student movement, he was elected to the National Union of Students' (NUS) national executive council. He spent time visiting picket lines and supporting worker struggles. While a PhD student, he organized against casualized contracts as a UCU member, and he has been on strike with UCU many times since. Jamie got involved with the IWGB during the first strike of Deliveroo riders in London. He then became secretary of the University of London branch, supporting strikes and in-house campaigns, as well as opening the branch up to other universities in London. Following that, he was elected as the union's branch support officer, helping branches to organize and run campaigns. He now oversees the General Members branch, which helps workers kickstart organizing in new industries.

We have been involved in many strikes with the IWGB and other unions, striking ourselves or supporting other workers' organizing efforts in universities, cleaning companies, courier services and many other places. There are two things that come up again and again. Strikes are almost always about dignity. They are a reaction to the way that bosses treat us as workers. Yes, we want more pay or better conditions, but we also fight for respect. Second, many of these strikes are about wresting control from management. They are about stopping work to get something, yes, but they are also, crucially, about trying to take some control back in our workplaces.

We have both seen countless so-called 'unorganizable' workers win, and this has deeply shaped our politics and the content of the book. In the UK, most worker organizing happens within trade unions, and while we've each organized as workers within and outside these bodies, they are where we have most of our experience, so the book will reflect that. However, we want to make a brief point about terminology in the chapters that follow. We will use the broader term 'worker organizing' to reflect the fact that the trade union form is not relevant everywhere. Either way, we are interested in worker organizing, whatever form this takes in practice.

It is worth noting that trade unions have played different roles in various countries. For example, in Brazil food delivery couriers march under a banner of 'motoboys unidos sem sindicato', which translates as 'couriers united without trade union'. This is because the Brazilian state mediates union membership. In some industries, dues were mandatory and taken as a tax by the government, then paid out to the union. While dues are no longer mandatory, many workers view unions as collaborating with the state. This means seeing unions as an organization that may not represent workers' interests. This does not mean there is no rank-and-file worker organizing, just that it takes different forms. While we may talk about unions in the book, we believe that the arguments in this book apply to worker organizing more broadly. We hope that readers can apply our key points whether they are members of unions or not.

The stories of organizing in this book have been chosen because they each highlight important aspects of how we can build power. We start with the examples of couriers organizing in the gig economy in Britain and waste collectors in Mumbai. Both cases of precarious workers show that no worker is unorganizable, and while many wrote them off, they found a way to fight back and win. We then discuss workers with quite different conditions – those at Kickstarter. Although not experiencing the same precarity, they fought for and won control at work. In thinking about how we can win big, we examine cleaner organizing at the LSE and St Mary's Hospital. We look to the sans-papier workers in France to show us how we can demand more at work, and then we delve into the water wars in Cochabamba, Bolivia, to learn how we can fight beyond the workplace. We look at the role of solidarity and the fight against oppression, along with the different ways workers have fought for liberation. We envision a bigger horizon for workers' struggle: not only fighting for more at work, but what it looks like when we demand control over our lives.

Taking the lessons from these various struggles, we want to involve as many workers as possible in our struggles. The book you're holding is not a how-to guide, but a set of principles that can guide our organizing as socialists. Because it is not only about winning, but also developing the confidence to build another kind of world.

I
THE TROUBLEMAKERS

Being a troublemaker is about trying to build power at work. Building power is always a process. It requires bringing workers together, developing confidence and discerning ways to win. Getting organized at work has immediate and obvious benefits. On average, if you are a union member, you get paid more and have better terms and conditions. This 'union wage premium' varies across industries but can mean substantial increases in pay. These benefits are the result of having increased power: bargaining as part of a collective is more effective than trying to bargain on your own. There are also protections and rights from union representation that make work less precarious.

In this chapter, we introduce a series of examples of workers organizing – and even as we wrote this book, events unfolded that offered further inspiration. At the end of 2021, the first corporate-owned Starbucks store in the US voted for a union. Since then, hundreds have voted to unionize, and hundreds more are petitioning for union elections. Amazon, which has long been a holdout against unions, saw a vote for a union at a warehouse on Staten Island. Workers organized an independent union, the ALU (Amazon Labor Union), winning against the full weight of Amazon's anti-union efforts. In the UK, the biggest rail strike in thirty years saw workers walk out on the London Underground and Network Rail. There were big pickets and rallies, bringing trains to a grinding halt. The secretary-general of the National Union of Rail, Maritime and Transport Workers (RMT), Mick Lynch, demonstrated how to use media appearances to assert a confident pro-worker and pro-union stance, winning more support for the campaign. It is an exciting time to be interested in troublemaking, with plenty of examples of what effective trouble can look like today. We have chosen a series of examples for this chapter that each tell us something about what we can achieve when we start organizing.

Even if you could find the perfect workplace, complete with excellent terms and conditions, you would still need a union there. As the experience of the Kickstarter workers discussed in this chapter shows, the only thing riskier than building a union is not having one. Those good conditions can be eroded over time, or things could quickly change if management decides they want to run things differently. It is important to remember that a workplace is subject to pressures and interests outside of it. That is also without factoring in global pandemics, the climate apocalypse and other factors that can dramatically reshape our workplace environments. We had no idea what the world would be plunged into as Covid-19 broke in 2020, particularly having so many people die through workplace infection. Power at work means having the power to say no. It is the power to say we will not work without the proper PPE (personal protective equipment) or keep doing something that will put us at risk.

This kind of defensive power is incredibly important to build at work. It can protect us and our co-workers. It makes work more bearable and it builds solidarity. But we also want to develop offensive power – not only in getting to say what we want to the boss, but in terms of demanding more. This can mean fighting to transform our own work, the workplace or society more widely. As we will discuss in this chapter, power at work is not just about improving the terms and conditions there – although it should do that too. It can be about having control over our working lives, then using that control to try and reshape our world more globally. If our movement is powerful enough, and we have enough leverage, there is no limit to what we can demand.

1

NO EXCUSES

Precarity has become a buzzword when talking about work. However, feeling precarious at work is something that many of us can long relate to. Precarious work is not just about employment contract instability; it can also mean there is little certainty about how much work you will get or whether your assigned hours will change. Bosses make our lives precarious in all kinds of ways. We feel it when we live paycheque to paycheque, unable to save because of low pay. We feel it when we are sick and cannot take the paid time off we need. We feel it when our right to live in a country is controlled by our boss. We may just feel it because that is how our boss wants us to feel: constantly grateful and happy for a job. We are told that there is someone else ready to take our place tomorrow if we do not perform, a warning that is not limited to low-paid jobs.

When we talk about precarity we are often describing a set of material conditions that add up to create a dubious reality. However, precarity is also a mindset that bosses try to create in us. As they strive for further profit or stretch out funding, workers' pay stagnates or falls and job conditions get worse. When we feel under attack and at risk, this precariousness makes work and organizing feel harder to do.

The first example that we want to introduce is the struggle of medical couriers in London at TDL (The Doctors Laboratory). It is a story about precarious work, but also about how that can be overcome. We spoke to Alex, who worked as a courier at TDL and kickstarted organizing efforts there. The company had hired Alex and his fellow medical couriers as 'independent contractors', which, in theory, meant that each courier was their own little business of one, contracted by TDL. They still had to wear a TDL uniform, work exclusively for TDL and quite literally had their work 'controlled'. Of course, when one company pays another for their services, they do not include paid time off, sick pay or a pension in the arrangement. This is a contractual trick that has long been used in the construction industry, but it is becoming increasingly commonplace across the so-called gig economy. The claim is that this creates flexible work. Undoubtedly, many of the couriers that Alex worked with were looking for more flexible ways to work, away from the strict rules of traditional employment and all the problems this can involve.

Every morning at 8:30 am, Alex called in to his 'controller' and they started sending him jobs. As a courier, his controller quite literally had the ability to control his week – and how exhausted he was at the end of it. If he was not on their good side, they could send him back and forth across London, cycling miles for low pay. The work was physically gruelling. Alex was in and out of clinics and hospitals all day, collecting medical samples and dropping them back at the lab in central London. Alex and the other couriers took pride in weaving in and out of traffic, completing jobs as quickly as possible to up their pay. Sometimes the benefits of working out on the road were obvious and other times less so. On mornings it rained, Alex was soaked to the bone by the time he reached the end of his street, yet he had to endure eight-hour days of riding with soggy socks in treacherous conditions.

Alex started organizing after a particularly hot summer week when the company was understaffed. He asked for a bonus, given the extra work they were covering. The manager agreed to this, but the bonus never materialized. The couriers knew the money was there, as their work was lining TDL's pockets. But at that point none of the couriers were convinced they could force the company to pay them anything extra.

There were many barriers to organizing at TDL, including language. Across the company's workforce, there were migrants from all over the world. The majority of couriers were Brazilian migrants who spoke only Portuguese. Despite their different backgrounds, they were all united in an experience of precarious work in London. There was a strong feeling that even by asking for something small they could risk losing everything: 'Don't bite the hand that feeds you.' The fear that any action could negatively affect them was part of the precariousness of the work, created and pushed by their bosses. It was not so much that they did not know how to make a change, but rather that achieving lasting change simply did not feel possible.

Without knowing much about what a union is, Alex started to try and improve his own conditions of work, alone. He went to the managers to discuss low and inconsistent pay. He was able to win some small improvements, but quickly found he hit a ceiling by being just one person, asking nicely. Through contacts in the courier scene in London, he joined the IWGB (Independent Workers' Union of Great Britain), a small, grassroots union of precarious migrant workers. However, he did not start organizing straight away. He felt it was important to join out of solidarity, as he felt his conditions were better than others. Soon he realized that didn't matter and that they desperately needed a union. It took a while, until, as Alex has explained: 'I decided it was time to call on the help of my union: the IWGB. Until then I had thought that there were so many couriers in London in worse-paid, more precarious situations than myself and believed that they deserved more urgent attention.'[1]

With the backing and support of other courier organizers, the movement to unionize at TDL multiplied. One union member turned into two, then ten and then the majority of the 150 workers. In every spare minute Alex had, he spoke to co-workers. It was not long before the collective organizing, even in such a hostile environment, showed benefits. As Alex described:

When you're on your own a knock back can be enough to shut you up and make you give up for six months to a year. But when you're part of something that's pushing, you get knocked back and there is someone else there to take up the baton or pick you back up. And you just keep going.[2]

The IWGB, although a young and small union, had a history of successfully organizing migrant cleaners and couriers. Alex and a few co-workers met with other workers from the union and began to plan a campaign. They put together a strategy to recruit across TDL, fight for trade union recognition, and launch an employment tribunal claim to challenge their bogus employment status. Alex described what happened after his co-workers voted to launch a campaign against TDL:

The next day, I arrived in the loading bay with the rest of the couriers. I was met with mixed emotions. Some couriers felt elated that someone was finally standing up to their long term abusers, pushing for justice for the courier fleet. Those who felt like this did not take much convincing to join the union. They were ready to start our fight for recognition and rights. It was not so easy with other couriers. Some felt what I had put into motion could cost them wages or even their jobs. At first, their fear manifested as animosity towards me. Couriers who had spoken to me every day since I started at the company turned away when I walked past them or muttered things under their breath. As you could imagine, these couriers were harder to convince to join the union.[3]

It took sustained organizing to show other workers that joining the union could be a way to improve conditions at TDL. They took on individual cases where workers were being treated unlawfully. There were highs and lows along the way. There were some victories, and other times workers cancelled their union membership, scared off by management intimidation.

Still, their numbers continued to swell. Eager to win big changes, the workers called a strike over pay and conditions. Strikers targeted the TDL office on the first day, waving the red flags of their union and storming the loading bay from which the controllers ran TDL's logistics. Alex remembers looking back up the ramp he had gone down for years to deliver samples and seeing a 'red river' of workers, angry and demanding to speak to the bosses. Strikers celebrated the strike with a motorcade, strapping flags to the back of their motorbikes and zooming off to Harley Street (London's private healthcare centre). Visiting the clients of TDL was a key part of their strategy, but seeing how empowered the workers were, Alex said it felt like more of a celebration.

Despite having almost no resources as a union, the TDL couriers used every tool they could in this campaign. They held loud and disruptive strike action, took legal action through the courts and got backing from MPs. Despite countless attempts from TDL to intimidate them, the workers used their collective voice to inform TDL's clients of the company's conduct. During one part of the campaign, they even got hundreds of supporters to write to more than a thousand email addresses linked to shareholders of TDL's parent company.

They shook the tree, and for a while no fruit came down. But they shook and shook and eventually things did begin to fall. These little wins eventually snowballed into the most successful gig economy campaign in the UK. In less than two years, they had reached a membership density high enough for the courts to force TDL to recognize them as a union. This was the first union recognition deal in the gig economy. The tribunal also ruled in their favour, offering either employee contracts or limb (b) worker contracts to couriers.[4] This won them holiday pay, a pension, a right to the minimum wage and so much more. It only took two days of negotiations for Alex and the union to secure a deal guaranteeing that all workers would receive a pay rise and a decent wage – their fate would not be left to the controllers anymore. They won fifty pence more per hour, paid mileage, an end to zero-hour contracts, a 12.5 per cent enhanced rate for night work and an annual pay review. We believe this is the biggest improvement in pay and conditions ever seen at TDL – or any courier company in the so-called gig economy with IWGB members.

Over the past two years, TDL couriers have seen a wholesale uplift in treatment. Instant dismissals are gone, management has to be polite to workers and the toxic atmosphere has lessened. Pay errors are less frequent and resolved faster, they now have twenty-eight days' paid holidays per year, paid mileage to cover expenses and a better hourly rate to reflect their hard work. TDL is no longer hiring couriers on a self-employed basis and has committed to fully fund the equipment, insurance, vehicles, fuel cards and other items needed for working under an employee contract. Couriers no longer have to shoulder the costs of work, including the £4,000 per year congestion charge for self-employed van couriers.

Alex and his co-workers described their struggle as shifting how they saw the world, like the moment when the Matrix is shown to be an illusion. The successes showed that real change is possible and that the couriers had real power. As Alex explained:

> As part of a community of riders who were fighting for better conditions I became aware of what can be achieved through collective action. Having felt like I was struggling alone for so long, it was incredible to be part of a group of couriers who were not tolerating exploitative conditions any more. Beyond the couriers branch, I became part of a union that was fighting back in an array of industries and I was inspired by the unity of workers, from cleaners to games workers, from security guards to foster carers. Now my eyes have been opened to this way of organizing and a collective way of trying to make a difference to so many, there has been no turning back.[5]

Someone who has felt this power is the boss's worst nightmare: They are now a troublemaker.

Misclassification and precarious working conditions are not unique to couriers, nor are they only found in the UK. There is no shortage of precarious workers in India. Around 93 per cent of all employment in India is informal. Against this backdrop, there are some workers who are more precarious than others due to the caste system. We discovered a powerful example of worker organizing when we met an Indian organizer, Milind Ranade. We invited him to participate in a panel at The World Transformed festival, speaking alongside representatives from other struggles.

Milind had been organizing with waste collectors since starting KVSS (Kachra Vahatuk Shramik Sangh) in 1996, a union for these workers in Mumbai.[6] Waste collectors, or manual scavengers, work in rubbish dumps or sewers. As Milind explained, 'the ancient caste system still dictates a person's occupation in India, and for Dalits, it means a life of dehumanising work as manual scavengers.' Dalits are the lowest caste, historically labelled as 'untouchables' and widely oppressed. Many thousands of Dalits work as manual scavengers, despite this being illegal under Indian law. Milind notes that 'even the state does not care about them'.[7]

The work is incredibly difficult. For manual scavengers, it involves going into the sewers and removing debris that is clogging the pipes. Workers have to contend with exposure to the waste, fumes and injuries while moving through sewers without safety equipment. One organization estimates that nearly 2,000 manual scavengers die every year in the sewers.[8] Unlike other forms of work where workers may have the possibility of other employment, this is not an option. As Milind explains: 'If Dalits quit scavenging, how will they afford a life? Even today, the community is expected to clean faeces – even as members of other castes would prefer unemployment over this humiliating work . . . There are cases where Dalits have set up grocery shops in villages, and no one has come to their stores since they're untouchables.'[9]

This could sound like the perfect example of 'unorganizable' workers. They lacked contracts, they were very badly paid, workers' conditions were so bad that many were dying, and they were socially excluded and oppressed because of their caste. As Milind explained, he first met these workers when he saw them sitting on top of the waste trucks. They were forced to ride on top of the trucks as no buses would agree to carry them. They faced major barriers to organizing. Social workers would try to help them by advising them to find other jobs, while trade unions simply refused to respond to them. Many of the workers are illiterate and have migrated to cities where they do not speak the local language.

Milind was an outsider trying to support these workers to organize. At first, they refused to engage with him. He kept going back to the dumping ground each morning and trying to talk to workers. It took two weeks before any workers would communicate with him. As he explained, 'after all, they had the right to be angry with us; to refuse to talk to us. What had we ever done for them? This system had been in place for 18 years, but we had paid no attention to them in all this time.'[10] Milind began using sign language to communicate with workers. Over nine months, he earned their trust and was allowed to travel with them on the garbage trucks. It took another six months of talking to workers about their rights and conditions to start organizing. They launched a new kind of trade union, KVSS, that focuses on waste collectors.

In addition to the challenges they faced, the workers were also part of a complicated system of subcontracting. The first campaign that KVSS undertook challenged this in a dumping ground in a suburb of Mumbai. Permanent workers had one entrance, while contract workers had a separate entrance. Contract workers had no access to water for either drinking or washing. Instead they had to buy water themselves. Members of KVSS organized a hunger strike for access to water. The campaign was taken up by the media and the workers won the strike after 24 hours. As Milind explained: 'workers got the confidence that yes, we can win something. And that water was a platform on which we built.'[11]

The city agency responsible for sanitation, the BMC (Brihanmumbai Municipal Corporation), had introduced subcontracting as a cost-cutting measure in the 1990s. Private contractors would be paid 1,200 rupees for each truck that collected rubbish from across the city and took it to a dumping ground. As one reporter explained:

The contractor would keep 600 rupees and give 600 rupees to a truck owner for the trip. The truck owner would keep 250 rupees for himself, pay 200 rupees for diesel, 20 rupees for a BMC supervisor known as a *mukadam*, and then give 40 rupees to the driver and 30 rupees each to three workers. So for 20 trucks, the contractors were making 36,000 rupees a day and each truck owner was making about 750 rupees a day for doing nothing, while the workers earned only 90 rupees a day for 12-hour shifts. The contractors had to pay up to half of their profits to BMC officers in bribes, thus creating a tight circle of exploitation and extraction of profits at the expense of workers.[12]

This is a powerful example of how subcontracting involves increasing layers of people looking to make a profit, heavily squeezing the workers who are actually doing the work. The workers of KVSS launched a campaign against this contract system. They started filing legal cases against the BMC, claiming that the contracting system broke Indian labour law. They sought to demonstrate that the BMC was responsible for them, particularly in cases of accidents or injuries. The court ruled in the workers' favour in 2003, making 1,200 workers permanent. As is often the case, however, the employer did not rest after being defeated in court. BMC decided to reorganize the work into a new contract system, adopting the so-called 'Hyderabad pattern' of contracting. This involves issuing contracts for only eighteen workers, as the Contract Labor Act applies to businesses with more than twenty workers. Workers are not called workers, but instead 'volunteers', receiving an honorarium rather than a salary. Contracts last only eight months, as the law allows workers to claim permanency after 240 days of continuous work. This system is clearly designed to evade labour law, but Milind also claimed that it was comparable to the Hindu law of Manusmriti, which excluded Dalits: 'the Dalits who were kept outside the boundary of the village are now kept outside the purview of the act.'

The workers launched a campaign against the Hyderabad pattern, building a case that they were indeed workers. They launched a 2007 legal campaign, which was finally won in 2014 and 2,700 workers gained the right to permanency. Again, BMC sought to challenge the decision. They rejected 2,400 workers, claiming that there were discrepancies in the spelling of their names. It took until 2018 for the union to force BMC to verify the rejected workers.

While these legal strategies demonstrate KVSS's successes, it was not the only tactic that the union used. Like the IWGB campaign at TDL, they combined different actions in their fight. However, they also engaged in some practices that are not part of our organizing toolbox in Britain. One of these is the 'body procession'. This involves taking the body of a worker who had died to the BMC headquarters. Bringing relatives and other workers, they marched on the employer they held responsible. Unsurprisingly, BMC was not keen on this kind of tactic, working closely with the police to prevent body processions. As Milind explains: 'in Indian society, if you are alive and if you are starving, nobody is bothered. But if you are dead, then everyone is scared because the emotional tempers can go high and anything can happen.'[13] The tactic taps into these fears, as well as providing a very public display of the risks that workers face in the job.

The union regularly engaged in other protests and direct actions to achieve their goals. These actions were part of mobilizing workers and building their confidence through the struggle. Milind explained how they 'went to the court.

We kept up our agitations. So it was a double attack. In the field, tremendous agitations, demonstrations. For each and every thing.'[14] The long struggle of these workers showed that despite being excluded, discriminated against and treated as less than human, they could build power at work. BMC has been forced to pay workers not only new rates but also back pay. When reflecting on the journey from being unorganized to powerful, Milind said, 'they never thought that such an unknown entity, without the backing of politicians, without affiliations to any political party, would succeed.' The story is one of patiently building power as workers, something that Milind 'credits his experience in the communist movement with teaching him how to fight and how to sustain a long, drawn-out struggle'.

The struggles of precarious workers in each of these cases show us that even the most precarious workers can overcome significant barriers and challenges to find power at work. The challenges of precarious work can perhaps be distilled into the aphorism that 'workers will not risk rocking the boat'. While precariousness can indeed create that kind of fear, it can also mean that there is less to lose – and so much more to win by rocking.

2

FIGHTING FOR CONTROL

While there are powerful examples of organizing with precarious workers, troublemaking should not be seen as limited to low-paid work. We have each heard many times from workers in both blue-collar and white-collar jobs that 'things aren't really so bad here' or maybe that 'it would be better for me to help someone else who has worse conditions than mine'. Those in 'good' jobs may perceive themselves as having much more to lose by organizing. Workers may have a more friendly relationship with management or currently enjoy some benefits at work. We very rarely talk about stable work also being a potential barrier to organizing. However, it too can potentially create a mindset that can damage organizing efforts.

German Lopez worked for Vox Media, which owns *New York Magazine*, *The Verge*, *Polygon* and more. In what he now dubs his 'worst tweet of all time' he said, 'I am against #VoxUnion.' He went on to say, 'I am generally fine with and even supportive of unions. Just not this one.' In 2019, he wrote a piece reflecting on the thread of tweets. He had previously said that he was worried that 'lazy' workers would use increased protections at work to keep their jobs. He believed that in 'high-skilled' industries, workers could use these skills as leverage to rebalance corporate power and advocate for themselves. His co-workers organized the union anyway. After witnessing their outreach and good organizing work, German explained that he changed his mind and joined.[1]

Anti-union rhetoric is so successful that it has some of us thinking that unions 'just aren't for us'. Those of us who have more 'professional' or white-collar jobs have been tricked into thinking that the way we can get ahead is through negotiating on our own. This might be by doing well in performance reviews, well-worded emails and asking nicely. Whether this comes from arrogance or a sense of superiority – or from never having won anything collectively – it undermines the idea of a union. For some, negotiating on their own may well reap rewards – although through pay inequality data we know this will mostly not be the case for women and people of colour.[2] It may get us a pay rise here or there, but it does not build power and it certainly does not win big.

Kickstarter is an online platform that hosts campaigns for crowdfunding, often involving creative projects. After Kickstarter workers started a union drive, the CEO published a statement. Aziz Hasan, the CEO, explained that 'the union framework is inherently adversarial. That dynamic doesn't reflect who we are as a company, how we interact, how we make decisions, or where we need to go. We believe that in many ways it would set us back, and that the us vs. them binary already has.'[3] However, that binary already exists in the workplace by the very nature of the employment relation – the economic relationship of work is adversarial, between workers and the boss, whether there is a union or not. The boss might be a lovely person or horrible. You may get on really well with them or not. This is not what creates an adversarial dynamic; rather, it is the different interests that each side has. The interests of the boss lie in a division of labour that rests on exploitation.

Bosses in many professional jobs have tried to convince us that because we work in an office instead of a factory, the relationship has somehow changed. They may claim that the greater responsibilities or say over parts of our work mean that we all share the same interests. This sort of argument has been weaponized by bosses to try and prevent worker organizing before it even starts. 'Unions are adversarial', they claim. 'They will disrupt the workplace and relations in it.' 'Unions are only appropriate for workers in some kinds of work or with particular problems', and so on. Such arguments are common in the tech industry, especially in the US. As the Kickstarter workers launched their campaign, the leadership of the company waged a covert war against them. They tried to use a nuanced argument, spreading the idea that 'we support unions, just not here'.

Just as German Lopez said at Vox, this idea of union-focused NIMBYism is common. NIMBY – aka not in my backyard – is a phenomenon where people may support

something generally, but not if it affects them directly. For
example, someone wants a phone signal, but not a phone
mast near their house. Bosses exhibit classic union NIMBYism
when claiming to be progressive and pro-union in general,
but they are against the idea of specifically giving up power
to workers through a union at their company.

Union NIMBYism spread through Kickstarter management – and workers, too. As a generally progressive workforce, of course they supported 'blue-collar workers' having a
voice and a union. But Kickstarter very effectively created the
illusion that unions were not for tech workers. At one point,
they even weaponized the language of 'privilege' and 'appro-
priation' against them. Three co-workers sent round an email
claiming that they were 'concerned with the misappropriation
of unions for use by privileged workers, some of whom receive
compensation more than twice the average income in NYC'.[4]
Despite management's statement that unions were a good
force in the world, at the regular 'all-hands' meetings, the
management would bombard workers with anti-union
messages. They also tried positive persuasion: All of a sudden
they were available for one-on-one friendly chats, trying to
make anyone feel that they could raise issues, and they threw
lavish parties to celebrate the company.

The issues of apathy and individualism also came up at
Kickstarter. This is common across all fields, when someone
looks at their own conditions of work, does not see anything
wrong and so assumes there is no need to organize for changes
or to have a union. On the surface this may seem fair, but it

fundamentally misses the point of the union: power and solidarity.

If we start with solidarity, not everyone in the union needs to be outraged at their own issues, conditions or pay. However, they must be willing to support those who are. In any workplace, bosses may try the age-old tactic of divide and rule. They might give more to one group of workers but not others. This could be higher wages, more security or power. It could even just involve treating them differently. For those workers without immediate issues, the task is to look around, see who else is struggling and add your voice to theirs and amplify it. This might be a person you work closely with, the person who cleans your office at night, does the customer service, and so on. In many cases, this aligns with oppression in the workplace. Men, and mostly white men, are likely to have more power or security in a white-collar workplace, whereas those who have been historically marginalized benefit most from strong collective solidarity.

The spark that lit the tinder box at Kickstarter was a battle for power at the company, as well as a need for solidarity with marginalized voices both within the workplace and beyond. A comic book began fundraising on Kickstarter called 'Always Punch Nazis'. It was approved by the Trust and Safety team as being legitimate political satire. But after an outraged article from right-wing website *Breitbart* in August 2018, the management decided it was inappropriate and made the decision it could not fundraise on the site. This caused uproar among staff. The uproar turned to whispers of 'union', mentioned first only in quiet huddles of like-minded co-workers. The uproar reached such a crescendo that the decision was overturned, but retaliation from the company on those who were outspoken only further fuelled union chatter. The mission of the company that the workers were so keen to preserve was in jeopardy. Organizing was their route to gaining the collective power to safeguard it.

Despite their heavy personal investment in the company as a force for good, workers felt entirely at the discretion of managers' decisions. This was also felt keenly when Drip, a project that was almost ready to ship and had had considerable time and energy poured into it, was scrapped on a whim.

Kickstarter, despite being a B Corp (having an 'ethical' business certification) and generally 'progressive' company, fought the union drive tooth and nail. In a fantastic oral history of the union drive, a worker said, 'they don't just disagree with us, this is a war.'[5] Organizers battled the three common factors found in 'good' jobs; apathy, union NIMBYism and the 'things aren't so bad' mentality. Management developed these narratives and bombarded workers with them at regular all-hands meetings, with the help of an expensive PR firm hired to help them win the conflict. Despite the seemingly endless onslaught from management, organizers persisted. They tirelessly talked to their co-workers, organized with creators on the platform and spoke up at all-hands meetings.

After a year of organizing, it was time to vote to form a union. Workers visited a conference room at the New York office one by one to cast their ballot, overseen by observers from the union and management. One worker commented that it was the first time they had ever voted on anything in the workplace, their first bit of true democracy on the job.

Organizers gathered at their local office of the National Labor Relations Board (NLRB) in Brooklyn to listen to the count. As if choosing the most dramatic way to read the votes possible, counters produced votes one by one, parading them to the room and pronouncing which way the person had voted. 'Yes . . . yes . . . no . . . no . . . no . . . no.' Despite what seemed like an impossible number of 'no' votes, they won. After getting a majority of 'yes' votes, they now legally had to be recognized by their bosses as a union. Organizers poured onto the street, singing 'Solidarity Forever' and smoking cigarettes (despite many of them never usually smoking).

This victory came in February 2020, just weeks before all our lives got turned upside down with the onset of the Covid-19 pandemic. Facing huge redundancies, the union successfully negotiated much improved redundancy packages – going from two weeks' severance for every year of tenure to '4 months of severance, 6 months of health insurance coverage, 4 months of coverage for workers making over 110k . . . no non-compete clause, no non-solicitation clause, and . . . ensured recall rights so if the company wants to reopen these roles within the next year, they'll need to offer the spots to laid off workers first'. Clarissa Redwine, a former Kickstarter employee, said '*this* situation is exactly why having a union, and sustained, organized, collective, *worker* power is better than one-off concessions.'[6]

While the union won workers such huge improvements in redundancy packages, it was bittersweet. A full 40 per cent of Kickstarter workers were made redundant, seriously taking the wind out of the workers' sails. Organizers noted the bright side, though: workers from Kickstarter will likely wind up at so many different tech companies, spreading the word about unions further than they ever could before. Their victory at Kickstarter had shown not only that it was possible to have a union but why it was needed. They effectively fought the common misconception that collective action at work is only for 'low-skilled' or blue-collar workers and that unions are only for changes in terms and conditions. They showed that campaign goals should be far higher than how much we are compensated for work, but also about what happens at work. Workers who once fought against having a union at Kickstarter, when seeing its value in the redundancy process, changed their minds.

When reflecting on the process of unionizing and facing the frustrations of the NLRB process, one worker said, 'real labour justice comes from constant political activity and striking. Period.'

While these stories provide examples of where we have won, many still think 'we can't win big'. Even when the organizing gets underway, there will be many moments that you might think quietly to yourself that it is not possible or that it is just too hard. The bosses have resources, often plenty of them, while we may not have many. But even the biggest giants have their vulnerabilities. They all care about something that we have the power to disrupt. Whether that is their profit, their reputation, their shareholders or their festive party – by mapping and exploiting these weak points, anything is possible. In other words, we have got to be prepared to be troublemakers and take action to win big things.

3
WINNING BIG

Organizing with the cleaners at the LSE (London School of Economics) in 2017, we faced a multimillion-pound institution that had just about completely ignored the cleaners' union of choice: UVW (United Voices of the World). This only ignited the flames of what is the most fiery dispute we have ever been involved in. The cleaners, who were employed by the outsourcing company Noonan, demanded parity of conditions with staff employed directly by the university.

By employing the cleaners through a third-party contractor, the university legally avoided responsibility for their treatment and conditions. They were paid hardly enough to survive on, especially as the majority of cleaners were in their fifties or sixties and supported their families in London and abroad in the Caribbean or Latin America. Sick pay was a major issue, cleaners were only entitled to the statutory minimum – nothing for the first three days of sickness and then only £89.35 ($107) a week after that. Often, they would have to work through illness. In the case of one cleaner with a knee injury, supervisors tried to take sneaky pictures of her as she rested for a moment. Beverley, one of the strike leaders, summed up the situation to a meeting of students: 'We are in slavery. The only thing they have not done to us is shackle us and whip us. But by words we are whipped, by tools we use we are whipped.'[1]

The first organizing meeting that lydia went to was held in a hasty fifteen-minute slot between shift changes. The cleaners had taken over the canteen for their meeting, a place in which the university said they were not permitted to eat their lunch. Instead, they were relegated to the basement in a cupboard-like room. It was a crucial meeting to decide the next steps of the campaign. Petros Elia, an organizer and co-founder of UVW, had explained that in his experience they would only win if they were prepared to strike. Within five minutes, chants of 'Strike! Strike! Strike!' broke out – and strike they did! They held seven strike days in total and disrupted the campus with loud picket lines, Zumba classes, face painting and Bob Marley blaring out of speakers. There was tireless organizing work, students and workers together, trying to cause as much trouble as possible.

At a key juncture in the campaign, the cleaners had to decide whether they would call a strike on days students were taking exams. It would be a big escalation, causing disruption for a lot of people, but probably the people that LSE cared about the most. The strike days were called. When the day came, the cleaners led a loud procession around the campus, banging drums and blaring Reggaeton, outside of the buildings in which students were taking exams. The sounds of vuvuzelas and whistles pierced the otherwise silent campus. As expected, there was a backlash. Students complained to the management, demanding retakes and money back. That was when the victory came, taking us by surprise: we had won not only parity of conditions with in-house staff, but the LSE was going to employ the cleaners directly. Outsourcing was over and they had won big.

It created a domino effect. After the struggle at the LSE, fiercely fought worker campaigns erupted across London. As a result, SOAS, King's College London, Birkbeck, University of London, Goldsmiths University and the London School of Hygiene and Tropical Medicine all ended outsourcing. This victory sparked a movement beyond universities, too.

Almost every big win starts with a small one. At the LSE it was the sacking of three cleaners, or the 'LSE 3', as they became known. At St Mary's Hospital in Paddington, it started in 2019 with a rumour that had spread around the caterers, cleaners and porters. The rumour was that a couple of pennies was being deducted unfairly from their paycheques, resulting in a lot of money in total across the hundreds of staff.

Loreta came to the UVW office to discuss the rumour. A caseworker spoke with her about how it could be resolved through legal means. Petros, who was involved in the LSE campaign, overheard the conversation and was quick to discuss the possibility of starting with the lost two pence per hour but then moving on to fight for many pounds more an hour. Loreta left, having turned him down, thinking he was idealistic. However, the moment she got to the exit of the building she turned on her heels and marched back up to the office. She changed her mind and invited him to meet her co-workers at the hospital. She said, 'the first impression I was thinking, "Oh my God, I didn't know what does [it] mean, union", I've never been in a union office like that. I was looking for something more active, more supportive, not only for myself, for all people because we are all having a lot of problems.'[2] The problems extended beyond the rumours of deductions, including low pay, poor provision of uniforms and lack of vaccinations provided by their employer.

These issues are symptoms of a particularly nasty innovation of modern capitalism: outsourcing. Through the 1980s and 1990s, outsourcing boomed. Instead of hiring their cleaners, caterers and security guards themselves, major institutions hired them through an outsourcing company. These include companies like Sodexo, Noonan and G4S, which leach off institutions – often publicly funded ones like universities and the NHS – taking on multimillion-pound contracts and then passing on the bare minimum to the cleaners, caterers and security guards who actually do the work. As well as only receiving minimum wage, for the most part outsourced workers get the legal minimums for sick pay, holiday pay and pension contributions – far less than other workers who are directly employed and not enough to live on. In their widespread abuse and sexual harassment of workers, managers often exploit the fact that many workers do not speak the native language and may have irregular migration status.

At St Mary's Hospital, the outsourced workforce was made up of racialized migrant workers, in contrast to the mostly white management. Many of the workers were from the Philippines, Lithuania, Portugal, Sierra Leone and Brazil. Loreta, a Lithuanian migrant, said, 'nobody cares about the human beings and actually we want equality.'[3] The cleaners spoke out against the hospital. How could they keep in place a system that offers worse conditions to migrant workers and people of colour? It seemed like rank discrimination.

They were employed by Sodexo, a particularly nasty and incompetent company that paid just £8.21 per hour (almost $10). Instead of demanding better conditions within this outsourced arrangement, the St Mary's workers took inspiration from the LSE cleaners and demanded an end to it entirely. As Loreta later recalled, 'If somebody did it, why [could we not] do it? If nobody did it, let's go to try it. So [here I wanted to] actually do something which I never did in my life.'[4]

The recruitment drive began. Within weeks Loreta came back to the union office, a scruffy space in south London. It was stacked full of placards and banners, every corner filled with a desk occupied by a very busy caseworker. Its open-door policy meant the office was always a hive of activity, with a background noise level that left organizers shouting, often in Spanish, to be heard. Loreta came with fifty membership forms, all filled in and signed, and 'made it rain', throwing them into the air above the desks.

From there things happened very fast. Workers had joined with the expectation that they were going to be taking serious action to end outsourcing. They immediately demanded a ballot for strike action. Ignited by the possibility of real change, their numbers doubled again during the ballot period. Sodexo tried to defuse their anger, inviting the workers to negotiate with them directly. The workers refused. After all, Sodexo could hardly give the workers what they wanted: for Sodexo's contract with the hospital to end.

At this point, they were having union meetings at the hospital so big that they would just occupy rooms. Given the size of the meetings, managers were unable to say or do anything about it. Despite having a hundred workers in the room, each worker took their turn to declare why they wanted to strike, and each was met with cheers and whoops. 'I'm striking for my family!' 'I strike for dignity!' 'I'm striking for equality!'[5] Still, it was a fantastic surprise when the ballot results came back with a 100 per cent 'yes' vote for strike action on a 99 per cent turnout.

They coordinated strike dates with six other strikes of UVW members across universities, government departments and the royal parks. The strikes were just as raucous as their pre-strike meetings. UVW anthems from Bob Marley to Luis Fonsi's 'Despacito' became the soundtrack of their eight strike days. The music was only interrupted by drums, whistles and chants of 'Sodexo, Sodexo. OUT! OUT! OUT!' Despite heavy security and police presence, they defiantly stood their ground. Their power was palpable and there was a feeling of a movement being born. On one of the days, St Mary's workers visited the picket line of striking cafe workers on the other side of

London. The cafe workers were few in number, as it was only a small campus cafe. However, bolstered with the addition of the cleaners, they stormed the building, blowing whistles and vuvuzelas, leading to a quick victory for the cafe workers.

Then they reached a juncture in their own campaign. They had been on strike, occupied rooms and overall caused a lot of trouble and disruption. But still the management of the NHS Trust maintained their position: what they were demanding was simply not possible. Seventy workers led a silent occupation in the corridors to the hospital, sitting down outside the offices, refusing to move until they had a meeting with the Trust management. They succeeded in getting the meeting, but the message was still the same. The management told them that it was not within their power to give them what they wanted. Even if they had wanted to, it would take years of preparation and planning to end outsourcing. It just was not going to happen, or so they said. At this point, they started to doubt themselves – was this even possible? Had they been delusional?

But as one worker described it to us: they had started it, so now they should just give it everything they had. And if their demand was not met, after giving it everything they could, then so be it – at least they had tried. Another worker encouraged everyone at a meeting, 'I can see they are under pressure and at the moment we can't stop doing this until we get what we want. But I can see we are more than halfway through. The door is already open.'

Instead of shrinking back, they just went bigger. They threatened indefinite strike action. Workers spoke to doctors and the press, putting their stories out across social media and spreading the dispute to other hospitals. When the hospital put up fences to prevent them from picketing, they instead did a mass conga line around them. The workers disguised themselves and snuck into a town hall meeting organized by the Trust. Despite spending weeks on the picket line together, some of them did not even recognize each other behind the wigs, fake eyelashes and funny glasses. They took turns putting their questions to the management – how could they let such an injustice continue?

So disruptive were they that the Trust made the 'impossible' happen in January 2020, after just four months of campaigning. The workers had made it so difficult for the Trust to maintain the status quo of outsourcing that it was both easier and cheaper for them to move mountains and end outsourcing.[6] The practice was ended across all hospitals within the Trust, making 1,200 cleaners, caterers and porters direct employees of the Imperial College NHS Trust and winning them the same rights and benefits as every other NHS worker.

At the heart of it, organizing and winning is a simple game of maths. Can you apply enough pressure that maintaining the current arrangement is more costly to the employer (whether in finances, disruption or reputation) than making the change that you want? This was a simple but effective equation passed to us from Jason Moyer-Lee, former general secretary of the IWGB. Building that pressure is no easy feat, but this formula is one that we always come back to. Troublemaking, action and leverage are what allows us to win – and win big.

4

DEMANDING MORE

With organizing comes dignity and respect. Building a collective voice can make the boss listen to you. If you get organized, very organized, it can bring the ability to demand anything. Because of this, bosses, often with the help of legislators, try to limit what we can organize around and the demands we can make.

In the UK, technically, there is no legal right to strike – doing so involves breaking the employment contract. There are only some legal protections if the strike is organized following very strict rules. First, it must be part of a 'trade dispute'. This means it has to be about something between workers and their employers, focusing on one or more of the following: the terms and conditions of employment, termination or suspension of employment for one or more workers, the allocation of work, issues of discipline, the membership of a trade union, facilities for officials or trade unions, or processes for negotiation or consultation.[1] While this reads like quite a long list, each of these are quite narrowly concerned with the formal work process. Strike action on issues beyond this – whether 'political' issues or striking in sympathy with other workers – is not protected under the law. Even 'protected' strikes have to be organized by a union, with a costly postal ballot carried out by an independent body. There must be a turnout of over 50 per cent and then at least half must vote in favour. The union then has to inform the boss two weeks before taking any action.

In the US, requirements for a legal strike are even stricter. Most private sector workers are covered by the National Labor Relations Act. Workers can go on strike over an 'unfair labor practice' or for an 'economic strike'. Striking workers can be replaced permanently during an economic strike, while workers can get their jobs back at the end of an unfair labour practice strike. However, rail and airline workers can only strike over 'major' issues, farmworkers and domestic workers are not covered, federal workers do not have the right to strike, and for state and local public workers, it varies by state.[2]

The core activity of unions is negotiating the employment contract to get a better deal for workers, who are selling their time to a boss. However, organizing at work does not have to be limited to narrow economic demands. Bosses would have us believe that with our collective power at work we can only increase our pay or improve our conditions. That is simply not the case. It is also worth remembering the history of the labour movement. Unions have been illegal at various points and strikes have been severely restricted or banned. The labour movement has had to break the law many, many times. As the saying goes: 'there is no illegal strike, just an unsuccessful one.'[3]

The 'sans-papiers' movement in France is an important example of what other demands we can make at work. 'Sans-papiers' is the French for 'without papers', meaning migrant workers who do not have permits or documentation to work. In 1996, the French state introduced new anti-immigration measures, threatening to deport many workers. In response, more than 200 migrants took refuge in Saint Bernard's Church in Paris. The police attacked the church, forcibly removing and attempting to deport them. Deportation flights were arranged to Mali and West Africa, although some were prevented after local airport workers refused to unload aeroplanes.[4]

The sans-papiers movement grew from this moment, mostly through the mobilization of worker collectives struggling to regularise their papers. In 2008, a wave of workers across France 'decided to come out of the shadows and to demand publicly their regularization in launching an unlimited large-scale strike'.[5] The fight for regularization had shifted in France as legislation had changed. Employers could now request the regularization of a sans-papier worker by providing them with a formal job offer. Of course, few employers were prepared to do this, but it allowed for a challenge that could be won through direct action against employers. Migrant workers occupied workplaces that included restaurants, building sites and cleaning companies, and these sectors became a focus for the sans-papiers movement. Their key tactic involved groups of sans-papiers workers agreeing to take turns targeting each other's employers together, turning up to occupy and protest until a worker was regularised. Once a victory had been achieved for one worker, they could move on to the next employer. This went on until they reached all of them.

Although not without tensions, workers began organizing with the CGT (Confédération générale du travail) and coalitions of other campaign groups. The CGT saw the potential to organize with these new groups of workers, particularly in sectors that were difficult to access, like catering, construction and cleaning. The dynamics of their struggle led to a particularly militant form of action. First, by going public, workers either had to win their struggles or they could face deportation and going back underground. Second, the connections within the migrant communities formed links across workplaces. Once workers had achieved regularization, many would still strike in solidarity with those waiting for their papers. By October 2008, 6,000 sans-papiers workers, mainly from North Africa, took strike action across Paris. The movement grew into a broader coalition, including Confédération française démocratique du travail (CFDT), Fédération syndicale unitaire, Union syndicale solidaires and Union nationale des syndicats autonomes (UNSA), as well as six associations: Ligue des droits de l'homme, Cimade, Réseau education sans frontières, Femmes egalité, Autre monde and Droits devants. Together these became the Collectif des 11, which negotiated directly with the government.[6]

The struggle is captured in the excellent film *Coming For A Visit* (*On vient pour la visite*). It opens with a handheld camera shot following a group of migrant workers rushing up a stairwell into an office, starting one of these occupations. The documentary shows the tension with the employer, the police (who are quickly called) and the union representatives. It follows workers trying to get their employers to sign the one-year contracts needed for regularization. The film ends – spoiler alert – with a worker getting their papers and the collective joy of victory over a boss who has to provide the documents. It then shifts to interviews with employers, in which one gives a fantastic account of what it meant to them:

> As soon as they know they have rights, they take a lot of liberties. And in particular they have spokespersons! Before, with tears in their eyes, they'd say they would do anything to have a job, but as soon as they discover that there's something happening that could make them good with society then they are ready for anything.

The sans-papiers movement became an unprecedented strike wave to demand regularization. However, it also built confidence across previously unorganized workers to fight for better employment conditions and for respect more widely.

The sans-papiers movement is a powerful example of how workers have fought to demand more than just changes in their own workplaces, especially since there are often many things that we want to change beyond the boundaries of our employment. For the sans-papiers, this was about status and regularization, but we could easily imagine other issues with respect to the state, our housing, our communities, our right to the city, public services, and so on. In another particularly striking example, worker organizing expanded from the workplace to a struggle over access to one of the basic rights of life: access to water.

In the early 2000s in Cochabamba, Bolivia, the community struggled over their access to water. Privatization had been creeping further into public services from the 1980s, but what took place in Cochabamba was much more forceful. The World Bank and the International Monetary Fund were forcing changes – so-called 'structural adjustment' – on many countries in the Global South. Much of this was about pushing the claim that privatization is more efficient, introducing economic incentives. Despite widespread evidence that privatization has not delivered this – you only need to look at transport or healthcare in the UK, US and elsewhere – water provision was privatised in Bolivia. It is an example of 'accumulation by dispossession', which David Harvey identifies as a key part of neoliberalism.[7] This is a process that involves taking wealth from the many (whether held in public institutions or public goods) and centralizing it in the hands of private interests. Put simply: it is a process of theft.

Cochabamba had been suffering from a chronic water shortage. Many people did not have access to the water network and there were many state subsidies. The Bolivian government auctioned the Cochabamba water system, with only one bidder responding – the Aguas del Tunari consortium of private and foreign interests, including the American Bechtel Corporation, won the forty-year deal for $2.5 billion. However, 'won' may be too strong a word, as they were not competing against anyone else. The contract gave them rights to meter the entire water network, including all water in the districts and aquifers. The deal also guaranteed the consortium a 15 per cent annual return on investment. They had been given this legal right to expropriate water after the Bolivian parliament rushed through new legislation.[8]

These changes were an attack on the right to water for people in Cochabamba. The first monthly bills arrived with costs that had doubled for many. Some workers now had bills that were a quarter of their monthly income. The consortium's manager, Geoffrey Thorpe, said that 'if people didn't pay their water bills, their water would be turned off '.[9] Protests were organized and a coalition formed: Coordinadora de Defensa del Agua y de la Vida (Coalition in Defense of Water and Life) – otherwise known as La Coordinadora.

The coalition was led by Oscar Olivera, a former machinist in a shoe factory. He had become the head of the Confederation of Factory Workers of Bolivia and then a national leader in the Cochabamba State Confederation of Workers. As Olivera reflects, the organizing for what became known as the 'water war' began five years earlier. It was an 'effort to reconstruct a social network, or the social fabric of solidarity, that had been destroyed by neoliberalism'.[10] This effort involved union leaders from the Cochabamba Federation of Factory Workers trying to understand the problems facing workers. The 'idea was to learn about the workplace realities faced not so much by organized workers as by laborers in the invisible sector', which meant they 'wanted to study the new world of work that was hardly seen or known'.[11] The union started to organize outreach on the streets and through the media, contacting many unorganized workers. The union office was in the main square of Cochabamba, providing a focus point for these activities. This brought them into contact with informal workers as well as campesinos (farm workers). Towards the end of 1999, they became involved in conflicts over water with irrigation farmers, hosting the campaign out of the union office. The launch of La Coordinadora 'responded to a political vacuum, uniting peasants, environmental groups, teachers, and blue- and white-collar workers in the manufacturing sector'.[12]

La Coordinadora demanded an end to the contract with Aguas del Tunari and the repeal of the water law. Mass protests were held in the city plaza, with barricades erected across the highways. Olivera addressed the crowds:

> Compañeros, it's become a fight between David and Goliath, between poor people and a multinational corporation. They have a lot of money, and they want to take away our water.

The protests were also joined by older and retired workers, called out from Olivera's union. As William Finnegan explained: 'for a great many Bolivians, the labor unions retain an association with a time when workers were organized and proud, and when Bolivia's railroads and airlines and mines belonged to Bolivians'.[13] There was a symbolism to this new fight against privatization being led by a union leader. However, the protests were quickly joined by campesinos, workers from the informal sector, students from the University of Cochabamba and street children.

Direct connections were made between the factory workers and the campaign. The Manaco shoe factory fired sixty union members on 12 January, the anniversary of the formation of the union in 1944. Bringing together the memories of historic union struggles with the current water wars, a twenty-four-hour strike was called. Five hundred workers rode bicycles from the factory to Cochabamba, a thirteen-kilometre journey. They 'rode down to tell them they should stop work and continue the water protest', making the point by blocking traffic, smashing car windows and forcing shops to close.[14]

The government responded with repression. There were pitched battles in the street as police attacked the demonstration. The air was thick with tear gas and chaos broke out across the plaza. As Olivera reflected, it was the first time that tear gas had been used in twenty years, the last time being during a massacre of factory workers in the same plaza in 1982.[15] The wave of protests intensified, with more and more of the city joining the campaign. The government responded by sending in the military. By February, pressure on the government had got so intense they committed to a rate freeze. But the protests continued and mass arrests followed, with many more protestors injured in clashes. In March, an informal people's referendum was held, with 69 per cent voting in favour of cancelling the contract with Aguas del Tunari. The protests continued to build in April and the government arrested the leaders of La Coordinadora, including Olivera. By this time, the protests had spread to other parts of Bolivia, including the capital. There were national demonstrations called by campesino organizations and most of the major highways in the country were blocked.

The government declared a state of siege, echoing the fears of the Spanish colonists. Again, demonstrations were held in Cochabamba. A plainclothes US-trained Bolivian army captain, Robinson Iriarte, was caught on camera firing into the crowd. He killed Víctor Hugo Daza, a seventeen-year-old student. The Aguas del Tunari representatives were informed by the government that they could no longer guarantee their safety, so they fled the city. The government then informed them that because they had 'abandoned' Cochabamba, the contract would be revoked. A new water law was immediately passed, 'written from below' by the people, and control of water was returned to the public utility company, Servicio Municipal de Agua Potable y Alcantarillado (Municipal Drinking Water and Sewerage Service).[16]

The struggle in Cochabamba is a powerful example of how organizing, both with unionised and non-unionised workers, can provide a strong base for a social movement that can defeat a government. As Olivera remarked, 'union-ized workers . . . because of their experience in labor strug-gles, contributed crucial tactics during the times of fiercest conflict.'[17] The water wars 'revitalized Bolivian social move-ments, bringing a sense of hope back into the struggle after the dark years of retreat', and this fed into later struggles.[18] On a visit to Britain, Olivera explained that

[m]any companies in Bolivia against which we are fighting are British. And the demonstrations are very passionate because it is about our survival. Here in Britain, people have to pay large amounts of money for water. Just as in Bolivia, privatisation deals are signed on the backs of the people.[19]

We learn from this example not just that we can win big when we organize as workers, but that we can demand anything. With our ability to hit both capitalists and the government where it hurts, should we be organized enough, there are no limits to our power.

5

FIGHTING FOR LIBERATION

The water wars became a focus of the global justice movement, with news of the struggle and solidarity being shared across the world. However, this is only one part of a rich history of solidarity in the workers' movement. Many governments today have recognised how powerful solidarity actions by one group in support of another can be. In both the UK and the US, regulations have specifically tried to prevent these kinds of political strikes or secondary actions because of their effectiveness. Political strikes involve withdrawing your labour for a so-called 'political' cause, perhaps targeting the government. Secondary actions, or sympathy strikes, involve withdrawing your labour to support another group of striking workers. Although both forms of strike are restricted, this has not always stopped them from happening.

For example, in 2005, Gate Gourmet, a company that provided in-flight meals at Heathrow Airport, proposed sacking hundreds of their workers. A thousand British

Airways (BA) ground staff walked out in solidarity. The unofficial strike action led to the cancellation of 700 flights during the busy summer holiday period. About 100,000 passengers were stranded. Both groups of workers were in the same union, the Transport and General Workers' Union (TGWU, which later became part of Unite), but BA had outsourced catering almost a decade before. The TGWU made an emergency motion to the TUC (Trades Union Congress, a federation of trade unions) annual conference urging the repeal of the UK law prohibiting secondary action like this. The Labour government refused to consider any serious reform.[1] Governments are still scared of this kind of action.

These tactics have also been used for international solidarity in the labour movement. In London in 1920, workers at the East India Docks in London refused to load guns onto a ship. As part of the Hands Off Russia movement, they wanted to prevent the guns being delivered to counter-revolutionaries in Russia. In 1973, dockers walked off on strike, refusing to load weapons onto ships to Chile following the military coup and killing of socialist president Salvador Allende. After the Pinochet dictatorship took over (supported by the UK government) workers at the Rolls-Royce factory in Scotland refused to work on parts for the Chilean Air Force from 1974 to 1978. The struggle is covered in the excellent film *Nae Pasaran*.

Throughout the 1980s, countless workers organized solidarity actions through their trade unions and played a supportive role in the struggle against South African apartheid. British trade unions supported anti-apartheid campaigns, including organizing a boycott of South African exports. While many of these campaigns involved trying to pressure the government or to change public opinion, there were also solidarity actions occurring at a local level. For example, in Portsmouth, NHS workers refused to handle medical supplies from South Africa, journalists at the International Publishing Corporation forced management to reject adverts from the South African government and workers at Ford stopped the import of pickup trucks that were manufactured in South Africa.[2] These were concrete ways that workers in the UK offered solidarity to the liberation movement in South Africa, which would later end the apartheid system.

During the 2003 movement in which more than a million people marched against the Iraq war in London, two train drivers refused to move munitions from a base on the west coast of Scotland. The workers stated that they were opposed to the invasion of Iraq, which Tony Blair's Labour government was about to embark on.[3]

More recently, there have been campaigns supporting trade unionists in Colombia, for freedom in Palestine and calling for Kurdish leader Abdullah Öcalan to be freed from Turkish prison, for example. Palestinian solidarity has involved boycott campaigns that are reminiscent of the struggle against apartheid in South Africa. As part of the BDS (Boycott, Divestment, and Sanctions) campaign, many unions have become involved in raising awareness of the struggle in Palestine and how workers in other countries can offer solidarity. In 2021, dockworkers at the Italian port of Livorno refused to load a shipment of arms for an Israeli company during the height of a bombing campaign against Gaza. Similarly, workers in Durban, South Africa, once the recipients of international solidarity, refused to load cargo from an Israeli ship – demonstrating how solidarity shown decades before can come back around to fight later injustices.

We have heard opponents of this kind of international solidarity ask the rhetorical question: What does this have to do with us? While the actions of dock or transport workers can have a clear impact, cleaners and office or healthcare workers have a much less direct connection with oppressive regimes, invasion or war. However, solidarity is about much more than only direct actions; it is also about raising awareness, expressing public support and building our own global bonds. Union discussions of these issues should also be about raising political awareness in our own communities. We want to fight for better workplaces, but also for a better world.

Practically, solidarity also turns the heat up on employers, giving their behaviour an international audience. Joining the workers' movement means becoming part of a community with networks that are national but also international, enabling us to send messages of solidarity and take action in support of other workers globally. When TDL couriers were organizing their campaign, as discussed earlier, we reached out to supporters in Sydney, where TDL's parent company is based. Within days we were in touch with four unions and worker movements, attending their meetings (virtually) to speak about our issues. Two weeks later, they grouped together to organize a car rally at the Sydney headquarters in support of us on the same day that couriers went on strike in London.

Whether we are supporting fights for liberation in other parts of the world, trying to stop the coming climate apocalypse, reinforcing that Black Lives Matter or working for a world free of gendered violence, we want to use one of the most powerful tools available to us: organizing at work and our ability to withdraw our labour. There have been many in the labour movement who have criticised international solidarity, but those critics have also said that issues around sexism, racism, homophobia, ableism and other forms of oppression are distractions from so-called 'real' issues. If there are any 'real' issues in organizing, these are the ones that affect workers and that we can fight. Of course this includes things like pay, but it should certainly not be limited to just that.

The UK introduced equal pay legislation in 1970, making it illegal to treat men and women differently in terms of pay and conditions at work. Of course, simply introducing legislation did not automatically change long-running inequality at work. At Glasgow's city council, the largest local authority in Scotland, workers had been fighting 'chronic' discrimination.[4] Starting in 2006, women working for the council in schools, nurseries, care, cleaning and catering began fighting a new job evaluation scheme introduced by the Labour Party. Rather than addressing gender pay inequality, the changes further exacerbated the differences.[5] This meant work that was typically undertaken by women for the council was systematically underpaid compared with men's work. Workers of the UNISON, Unite and GMB unions launched 18,000 separate tribunal claims and it took a strike of 8,000 women in 2018 to force the council to start settling the pay claim that went back decades. The women of Glasgow used their power to fight a huge injustice that affects thousands of women and people of colour. In the UK the gender pay gap is an estimated 15.4 per cent among all employees,[6] while the race and ethnicity pay gap varies; it can be as high as 23.8 per cent in London.[7] In the US, the gender pay gap is estimated to be 24 per cent,[8] while the race or ethnicity gap can be as high as 27 per cent.[9]

Over the past few years, systemic sexual harassment and gender-based violence at work has been exposed by brave survivors. On 1 November 2018, an estimated 20,000 workers at Google walked out in protest over the company's handling of sexual harassment cases. They raised demands to end forced arbitration, resolve pay inequality, revise reporting processes and produce a report on sexual harassment. Google ended forced arbitration – a contractual clause that requires workers to resolve disputes through an alternative dispute resolution process rather than being able to take legal action. The walkout sent ripples across the tech industry, shining a light on the culture of cover-ups for sexual harassment. It also gave a glimpse of what an organized tech industry could look like – as well as the urgent need for one.[10]

The following year, workers at Riot Games in Los Angeles walked out over the use of forced arbitration. An investigation found that there was 'rampant sexism' and a 'bro' office culture, with gender discrimination and harassment. After campaigns and legal action, Riot Games agreed to settle with a $100 million fund, sharing the payment out to every woman who had been employed at the company over the past five years.[11] In 2021, a lawsuit at video game company Activision Blizzard revealed a 'frat boy' workplace culture of sexual harassment and abuse.[12] The company fought the lawsuit. Workers organized an open letter in response, before later walking out in protest. The struggle against sexual harassment at Activision Blizzard has become a focus for worker organizing across the video game industry.

These high-profile actions have shown publicly how workers can collectively oppose harassment and abuse at work. However, for public events like this to happen there is much organization needed beneath the surface that builds the confidence and capacity of workers to stand up, and this kind of organizing is often not publicised. A joint initiative by the IWGB and UVW in the UK shows what this kind of activity can look like. The initiative brought together women, non-binary and transgender members from both unions as well as the Latin American Women's Rights Services (LAWRS) to run extensive consciousness-raising sessions, trainings and community-building events. The project focused on educating all union members on the dire state of gender-based violence in the UK, but it also built a roadmap for how to organize against it. In a country where only 1 per cent of sexual harassment in the workplace is reported to a union rep,[13] pushing this issue to the top of every union's organizing agenda is both crucial and powerful.

II
'SO, WHAT DO YOU DO?'

Think about what you had for breakfast. Where did all the parts for it come from? The bread, cereals, eggs or whatever it might be, along with the juice, milk, tea or coffee. Was there electricity for the lights? Was there hot water for a shower or bath? Have you travelled today? Think about how each of these different things have relied on the work of others, often in hidden ways. We often know little about the conditions under which all this work happened. It is quite certain that you did not prepare all these things yourself, farming and harvesting your own food, generating your own electricity, heating your own water, building your own car or laying the tracks for the train. Instead, you were able to rely on other people and things they have done to meet these needs. All these different forms of work had to come together in just the right way to prepare you for work. This is also true of the book you are reading now. You know who wrote it (as it is on the front) but who edited it? Designed the cover? Typeset it? Checked for errors? Printed the copies?

Distributed and sold them? How many people attended meetings, entered data, sent emails and so on, in order for you to end up with this book in your hands or on your screen? A lot of work had to happen in order for you to read this book about work.

We do not often think about the work hidden behind things like this book – or the struggles of workers that happen behind the scenes. In this second part of the book, we want to focus on the dynamics of work under capitalism. This means asking the question we often dread to hear at social gatherings: 'So, what do you do?' We want to ask this question critically, thinking about how figuring out our work is the starting point for understanding capitalism today.

6
WORK

Capitalism

Let's start by recalling the basics. Capitalism is not magic. Capitalists invest money to make even more money. They do this by making workers produce commodities for profit, capitalists pay workers less than they produce, taking the surplus for themselves. This process of production and exchange turns the money invested into more money. This is called capital accumulation.

A single capitalist has to compete with other capitalists, pushed into continual competition. They cannot choose to slow down the pace of work or pay workers more out of the kindness of their heart. If they do, another capitalist will undercut them. This means producing to sell for the most profit, regardless of whether this makes sense. Focusing on competing to produce in this way makes collective planning difficult. Instead, sometimes the state has to intervene to regulate or limit certain activities. For example, the Factory

Acts in the nineteenth century in the UK regulated employment by preventing children from working. This went against
the interests of individual capitalists, who protested the
changes. Since then, workers have fought for many regulations that have been introduced, including those for maxi-
mum working hours, the right to breaks and minimum wages.
These are victories for workers, but they also try to tame the
drives of capitalism in the short term to ensure a longer-term
sustainability.

Drawing attention to material interests is key to understanding capitalism and class as a system. Capitalists and
their political allies may well meet in private members' clubs
and scheme together, with glasses of whisky in one hand and
cigars in the other. But our system is not the result of a
conspiracy. Instead, through material interests, classes form
in struggle against each other. Material interests are objective
economic factors that influence us. For example, it is in the
interest of a boss to make a profit from a business. Making a
profit might line their pockets directly, make the company
they own more valuable (increasing their wealth), enable
them to pay higher dividends (increasing their wealth) and
allow for the expansion of the company (increasing their
wealth for years to come).

Workers, on the other hand, do not share the same material interest in the company. Mostly, workers do not automatically benefit financially when profits increase. We may get
cost-of-living increases, but in many cases wages are falling
due to inflation. For example, in the UK, the labour share of

income has fallen from an average of 69.9 per cent from the 1960s to 59.9 per cent today.[1] In the US, the share has fallen from around 65.4 per cent to 56.7 per cent.[2] However, we do have material interests at work. Given that we rely on our wages to buy the things we need, we have an interest in making more money, keeping more from what we produce, getting a promotion and so on. Material interests do not solely determine how people will behave, but they shape our actions and push us one way or another. Marx described the 'silent compulsion of economic relations'[3] to show that material interests operate in ways that are not always obvious.

Capitalism is obviously more complex than this in practice. It is more than just distinguishing between 'the exploiters' and 'the exploited', but our system still polarises these interests. These material interests are key to understanding work and class, and this understanding will aid you in your organizing. Your boss might be a nice or nasty person, but when the chips are down, they act in their interests as a boss.

Why Work?

Let us go back to an even more basic level. What even is work, really? Work is the capitalist employment relationship. At the simplest level, it involves us getting paid for doing a job. At the most complex it involves things as different as childcare, building houses, flying aeroplanes, growing vegetables and making PowerPoint presentations. It can become incredibly specific, sometimes involving many years of training. We prepare for work throughout our childhoods and are often judged by the work we do. Think of the terrible small talk question: 'so, what do you do?'

There are two quite different reasons for why we have to work. The first is that all people have needs. We interact with the world to meet our needs. This starts with the most basic gathering of resources and goes all the way up to the complexities of modern production and distribution. Think about the questions we started this part of the book with: what have you done already today? What kinds of work have you had to rely upon?

Unlike Robinson Crusoe, we cannot forage and produce everything that we consume ourselves. Instead, across society, our work focuses on meeting different wants and needs. This is the division of labour and it allows specialization. The results of this work can then be shared. For example, neither of us could have written this book without all the specialist labour needed to publish it. We also could not have survived in modern society long enough to do any writing without other people's work.

This sounds like a wonderful vision of why we work. It could give the impression that the world is made up of people cooperating, specializing in different ways to make sure we meet everyone's needs. But this is not how the world works in reality. We do not go to work to help everyone collectively meet their needs. We go to work to earn a wage that enables us to meet our needs. The things that we do often feel quite distant from meeting either our own or other people's needs.

It might be that you do an activity that is connected to one human need. For example, serving food, teaching or healthcare. Or you might do something that feels disconnected from meeting any needs. Maybe it is sending emails or changing numbers on a screen.

Under capitalism, we meet our own needs through buying commodities. A commodity is something external to us that allows for the satisfaction of a human want or need. It does not matter what a commodity is, only that it is something people happen to want or need. It could be a concrete product or a less tangible service: a pair of scissors or a haircut. As a system, the basis of capitalism is the production of commodities for sale, not finding a way to meet everyone's needs. Instead, commodities produced through work are sold for profit.[4]

This feature of capitalism is key to the second reason that we have to work. When we need to buy commodities to meet our needs, our ability to survive becomes tied to having an income. We need to pay to have somewhere to live and buy the food we eat. This leaves us a bleak choice: we are free to choose whoever we want to work for (as long as they will employ us), but denied any other way of meeting our needs other than going to work.[5]

Fundamentally, for almost everyone, we go to work because someone pays us to do so. We do not have control over what we make or do at work. We do not get to decide with whom our work is shared; instead, we get paid. We need that money to buy things that are the result of other people's work.

Time is Money

So what are the bosses paying us for, fundamentally? Labour-power (or the capacity to work) is the unique ability that we have to interact with and change the world. At work, labour-power creates commodities. When a boss hires us, they are buying our labour-power. When we get paid, we are receiving that money for giving over our time and capacity to work. While it gets dressed up in complicated ways, this is what work is. You sell your time as a commodity to someone else for money. This enables you to have the money to buy other commodities to fulfil your needs (and hopefully your wants). You sell your time and effort, but also give up control over what happens during that time. Think about that feeling you get just before work. If you work Monday to Friday, this is the dreaded 'Sunday night blues' – the feeling of the relative freedom of the weekend coming to an end too soon. Even if you like your job, the last day of a holiday always has that feeling. No more lying in or getting to choose what you are going to do for the day.

This is, in essence, what the employment contract involves. By signing the contract, you agree to someone else directing you and have them take control of your time. It is quite difficult, although not impossible, to turn up to work and do nothing (we have both tried). Regardless of whether you enjoy the job, there are opposing interests between the buyer and seller in this relationship. You want to get paid, but you also want to have some energy left for the rest of your time.

This is not an interest shared by your boss. When a boss employs a worker, they are buying the worker's labour-power like any other commodity. This means they want to use it to the greatest effect.[6]

This might not chime with your experience of work; we know that not everyone hates their job. Yet when we strip the relationship back to its economic core, it is unequal. Those selling their labour-power are at a disadvantage to the boss. In general, working much harder is not going to result in the boss paying you more. If working hard meant high pay, it would be the Amazon warehouse workers, not boss Jeff Bezos, making billions.

7
MANAGEMENT

When you think of exploitation, your mind may go to those of us who are struggling on minimum wage. It may go to those who work in terrible conditions. These are examples of particularly exploitative practices. But exploitation is at the heart of every relationship between a boss and a worker. This does not mean that some jobs are not more enjoyable than others, or that parts of work are not enjoyable, or that the wage cannot provide us ways to meet our needs, or even some of our desires. It means that someone profits from the surplus that we make or help to make. This relationship of exploitation is the basis of class in society. It involves workers producing things or services on one side, with bosses who appropriate the labour of workers on the other.

Class has many meanings. For some people, it is about a cultural identity. For example, the accent you talk with, the region you were born in, the kind of music you listen to or whether you drink flat white coffees and eat avocado toast. Class, however, cannot be boiled down to solely cultural identity. But that does not mean it is not important. As labour historian E.P. Thompson argued, 'the making of the working class is a fact of political and cultural, as much as of economic, history. It was not the spontaneous generation of the factory system . . . the working class made itself as much as it was made.'[1]

We, however, cannot make sense of class by only focusing on culture. Class is a social relationship of exploitation. This means classes only exist in relationship to each other. For example, there could only be lords because there were serfs, like there can only be bosses because there are workers. It is a relationship of exploitation that builds upon and extends to other forms of oppression. Oppression and exploitation combine in our individual and collective experiences. Gender, race, religion, sexuality, migration status and disability are critical to our experience as workers. These are not distractions from talking about class but are crucial for understanding struggles between classes.[2] While oppression existed before capitalism, it has continued to play a key role in the development and maintenance of capitalism. Oppression serves to reinforce the interests of those in power. Race, for example, is a social relation. Racism has been used to justify the slave trade, colonialism and imperialism. It has no objective basis, but it is used to create differences and divide people. These boundaries can also change, as seen in understandings of who is 'white' in the US, which have changed over time.[3] Various forms of racism can intensify based on specific events, too, like the rise of Islamophobia during the War on Terror.[4]

Class today brings together people with a wide range of experiences, united in having to sell our labour-power to bosses. In the UK, around 31 million people are in employment out of a population of around 68 million. In the US it is around 151 million out of a population of 332 million. Out of a global population of around 7.9 billion people, there are roughly 3.4 billion workers. There are many people trying to find employment too, retired workers and even more young people who have yet to become workers. It is what most of us will do for most of our lives.

Bosses

At the time of writing, Jeff Bezos, the founder of Amazon, has accumulated £140 billion. If you went to work at an Amazon warehouse in the UK it would take over 8 million years to earn that much money. Bezos sits atop a pile of wealth so large it dwarfs even the fantasy tales of dragons sitting on heaps of gold.

What does Jeff Bezos actually do? Bosses – capitalists – use money to try and make more money. Someone becomes a capitalist boss when they buy the 'means of production' and then employ others to work for them. Take a call centre, for example. The boss pays for the office space, the equipment, the headsets, the software, the numbers to call, the bills, and so on. This is the 'means of production' for a call centre. On their own, all these things would just collect dust. Bring a worker in and they can start making calls and selling things.

The boss is only going to employ people if they can make those sales. This means bringing in more workers to make paying for the workplace worthwhile to the boss. It also means only keeping workers who are bringing in enough sales. They need to at least cover the costs of their own wage and the means of production. To make sure this happens, the boss also hires supervisors and managers, who ensure the people are working hard. In the call centre, it is also possible to start timing and tracking workers. This supposedly makes that task easier.[5]

In this example, the boss only employs workers who can 'produce' more sales calls than they cost in wages. Imagine the call centre is selling something for £5. If the boss pays workers £10 per hour, they will need to make at least two sales per hour to cover their own wages. On top of that, they need to cover the costs of the means of production as well. Once their work covers these costs, any other sales would result in a surplus. If a worker only made one sale per hour, it would not make any sense for the boss to employ them. No one runs a call centre because it is a fun thing to do. If there was not any extra value produced in the process, the boss could not make any profit for themselves. Indeed, they might even have to hit the phones alongside workers to survive – imagine!

Think about how this relates to what you do. The work you do might be easy to quantify and you know exactly how much a boss is profiting from your work. For example, many outsourced workers can find out how much their employer is being paid. Outsourcers may charge £20 per hour to provide a cleaner, but only pay £9 per hour in wages.

On the other hand, it may be much harder to see this. Many different kinds of work go into ensuring that bosses can make profits. Teachers prepare the next generation of workers (and provide childcare while worker-parents work). Doctors ensure that workers are fit to work. Even where these workers might not be directly exploited by a boss, their work helps keep the entire system afloat, with healthy and educated workers ready to sell their labour-power. Other people work to pick up the pieces of a profit-driven economy.

And there is plenty of work that looks as if it is outside of capitalism altogether. The nuclear family, often considered to be a natural relationship, emerged with capitalism.[6] It is vital to remember that there would be no workers without the unpaid labour of the family. As Mariarosa Dalla Costa argued, 'where women are concerned, their labour appears to be a personal service outside of capital . . . she is always on duty, for the machine doesn't exist that makes and minds children.'[7] To be ready for work, we need rest (at least some), food and clothes. While these are our short-term needs, in the long term, the next generation of workers needs raising, care and education.

Outside of the workplace, we require care, housing, education, healthcare and leisure. Capitalism exploits many of these activities for free – we are not paid to look after each other or our families, for doing the cleaning, cooking and washing up. This is sometimes called 'social reproduction'. It involves the way we reproduce ourselves (make ourselves ready for work) and others as workers, both as individuals and as a class. It is clear that capitalism relies on much more than only paid work. It would grind to a halt without both paid work and unpaid labour.

Today, many people pay for parts of social reproduction. Rather than providing these activities ourselves, we can buy them from other workers. For example, think about working late. Takeaway food is an alternative to cooking, especially if the fridge is empty. Many parents send children to childminders so they can keep on working. Migrant workers clean other people's houses.

Capitalism today requires huge numbers of people to ensure that exploitation can continue. Some of you, however, may be thinking you have no idea how your job makes capitalism function. David Graeber identified what he called 'bullshit jobs'. He described these as 'a form of paid employment that is so completely pointless, unnecessary, or pernicious that even the employee cannot justify its existence even though, as part of the conditions of employment, the employee feels obliged to pretend that this is not the case'.[8] Instead of reaping the benefits of capitalist innovation by reducing the working week, our collective Puritan work ethic has transformed labour in the service of capitalism into an almost religious obligation and from which we get our self-worth as humans. Luckily, David's prescription for this mess is the same as ours: build unions and fight for better.

Whether you feel like your job is meaningful or bullshit, whether you enjoy it or hate it, it forms part of a wider system of work and capitalist production. Work is the capitalist employment relationship, defined by economic exploitation. It is the basic relationship of capitalism.

Managers

But even where we have an obvious boss, most of us are not directly managed by them. Indeed, we may have never even met the big boss. Jeff Bezos does not personally oversee the running of Amazon across the world. On a day-to-day basis, most workers interact with managers. Managers hold the interests of the company and the boss. Often managers' pay and performance connects to the interests of the company. This means they usually have an incentive to make us work harder. They are not sharing the profits in the same way as the boss, but they often get rewarded more than workers do.

One feature of modern capitalism is a huge growth in management. It includes more people in the workplace taking on aspects of managing other workers. For example, in many service jobs, the boss and upper management can be quite remote – so instead they may hire a supervisor who is only paid slightly more than the other workers. They have to make sure the work is happening.

This makes the power relationships less clear in the workplace. It also makes more people responsible for overseeing exploitation at work. Erik Olin Wright describes this managerial role as involving 'contradictory class locations'.[9] Managers have a contradictory position – they are both workers and the representatives of capitalists. They have to sell their own labour-power and may have surplus labour appropriated from them. But they also carry out the function of capital, controlling the work of others. They might take part in decisions about how to use the means of production or even what to do with the surplus. Within the category of 'manager', there is a lot of variation. For example, the supervisor in a call centre might control the schedule. They might discipline workers and try to encourage higher performance. However, they may get little say in the running of the call centre. At a higher level, senior managers who make strategic decisions are much closer to those who own the business.

Managers are an important feature of work. As we discussed, work is a particular relationship of buying and selling of people's time, and management occurs after that sale to make that time as profitable as possible. There is a long history of different forms of management, including tried and tested techniques to wring as much profit as possible from a set amount of our time.

Management is about control. It is about the conflict between your interests at work and those of your bosses. Control is always a problem in practice because workers are not machines. Unlike the other resources that managers might control, labour-power comes attached to people. People have their own interests, wants and needs. We also have the power to resist being treated like any other commodity.[10] Management control is always an 'attempt' rather than a given.

One infamous solution to this problem of management came from Frederick W. Taylor. His ideas later became known as Taylorism, the so-called 'scientific' theory of management. Taylor, the son of a wealthy family, chose to go and work on the factory floor. While trying to understand factory work, he developed an obsession with what he called 'soldiering'. Pulling no punches, Taylor argued that:

Underworking, that is, deliberately working slowly so as to avoid doing a full day's work, 'soldiering', as it is called in this country . . . is almost universal in industrial establishments, and prevails also to a large extent in the building trades . . . this constitutes the greatest evil with which the working-people of both England and America are now afflicted.[11]

This obsession of Taylor led to his development of 'scientific management'. He focused on the labour process. This is the way that workers' labour-power is directed towards making a profit at work. Taylor broke the labour process down into its constituent parts, then measured each part to see exactly how long it takes. For example, in the Midvale Steel Works, Taylor carefully measured each part of the labour process, from carrying coal and pig iron, to the turning of steel on the lathe.

Taylor was trying to capture the knowledge of the labour process that workers develop during the job. The idea was that managers could then use this knowledge against workers

for more effective control. After all, if they did not understand the work, how could they know if workers were using
the time most efficiently? Many managers share the same
fears that led Taylor to develop his theory, worrying that
workers are not putting in as much as they could.

No matter your workplace, we likely have all shared the
experience of having a manager who does not understand the
reality of what we do. Maybe they ask for a change that would
actually make our work slower. Perhaps they suggest something that is not practical. A great example of this is the reality TV show *Undercover Boss*. If you have not seen it, each
episode follows a simple formula. Something is going wrong
at the business. The boss decides to go undercover, donning
a questionable disguise. They start as an entry-level worker
in the company. They see problems with the organization of
work from the perspective of workers. Workers tell them
about difficult personal circumstances. Through doing the
work, they learn about a series of changes that could improve
the business. Finally, workers get called back into the head
office for the reveal. The hardworking employees receive
rewards and changes are introduced.

Taylor did not plan to reward workers. Instead, scientific
management turned the process of managing into a set of
principles. First, managers study the work process to try and
understand it like workers do. Second, management collects
this knowledge and keeps it to themselves. Third, this
monopoly on knowledge is used to try to control every step
of the work. This is important today because it involves 'a

theory which is nothing less than the explicit verbalization of the capitalist mode of production'.[12] Taylor's dream was that every workplace could undertake similar studies to his own, with managers taking the knowledge from workers and using it to fight soldiering. Attempts to do this have included consultants and time-and-motion studies, and ultimately, Taylorism has become a governing principle of managing work. It is now used by many bosses and managers to try and reorganize work over time. However, it is an expensive and disruptive process, and many workers have resisted the application of Taylorism, whether on the shop floor or by leaving the job.

A key part of these principles is separating 'conception' from 'execution' at work. This means taking away control of tasks from the workers who are doing them. It is an attempt at control by management, setting the pace of work in a way that hopes to prevent soldiering. A factory assembly line is one way of doing this. It involves centrally setting the pace, and each worker then has to keep pace as production moves through the factory. The automatic dialling and scripting in a call centre is a similar process. It controls the pace, with a new call starting the moment the previous one has finished. It also takes away much of the creativity of the work, providing the exact words to say. The principle of the assembly line is no longer limited to the factory – it gets applied to all kinds of work, from teaching to hospitality to care work, any instance where managers try to set the pace of work to prevent soldiering.

It is rare to hear today that management is about crushing the 'soldiering' of workers. While the terminology and techniques may have changed, the intention remains the same. It is much more common today to have an HR – or human resources – department. This is an odd way to refer to managing people. It gives the sense that workers are some kind of transferable unit of resource that is used by managers. Having developed from Taylor, HR often focuses on issues like recruitment, job design, pay and rewards, employee voice, performance management, appraisals, engagement, retention and turnover. Each of these issues still relate to getting the most out of workers' time, although it is now couched in 'cutting-edge', 'thinking outside the box' jargon focused on the need to 'circle back' for 'synergy' and to 'pivot' to 'blue sky thinking'. What they do not look at, of course, is whether workers should have to work harder to meet targets or be more engaged. HR is a new way for bosses to try to achieve the same things as Taylor. Management often presents HR as a referee between bosses and workers, but HR always works for the company, not workers.

In practice, management tries to develop new ways to check up on workers. It might involve filling out forms to track exactly what you have done at work. It could involve integrating productivity apps like Slack or online timesheets. During the pandemic there has been a huge growth of 'employee surveillance' software.[13] These claim to provide a way for managers to monitor workers remotely. They check whether workers are working from home, not slacking off watching Netflix. Taylor's old fear of 'soldiering' has returned, this time with managers who have many more technological options at their disposal.

Technology has long provided ways for management to try and control work. We are often told that technology is neutral or only the next invention in a linear process. Instead, different technologies are the result of struggles over alternatives. Technologies are designed, developed, created and used within existing power relations and they have the interests of those who make them written into them. This is, again, about the importance of material interests. Technology is often used to take control away from workers, whether it is machinery that sets the pace or online systems for tracking us, it provides another powerful tool for management.

Being managed at work may come in the form of a shouting boss, a manipulative supervisor, a friendly HR professional or via some new technology. Either way, the boss is interested in making workers perform effectively while at work. At the core, this is a problem of control. Workers are not software, machinery or commodities; we are complex people who have our own interests and can respond to these attempts to control us. Workers have thus developed different methods, strategies and tactics to wrest control back from management. The result of these different interests is workplace conflict.

8
CONFLICT

Conflict at work is a result of the push and pull between workers and management. We can think of control at work as a 'frontier',[1] like a line drawn across a map when armies skirmish with each other. Workers may win something in one area, but lose control to managers elsewhere. The line is drawn and redrawn as the result of the constant push and pull at work.

Often, workplace conflict is seen as a sign that something has gone wrong. Thinking about the different material interests we have discussed so far, conflict is in fact a natural and constant part of work. In practice, conflict takes many forms. Each shifts the frontier of control this way or that. It is not often that a workplace is either calm and happy or bursting with open conflict – there is much on a sliding scale between these two sides.

The CIPD (an HR company) notes that 'it's hard to pin down a precise definition of conflict, and one person's perception of a difficult situation can differ from someone else's'.

They explain how 'some conflict can even be positive', but that there is a 'wide spectrum of behaviour' that could count as 'negative'.[2] They include disagreements, personality clashes, or things like bullying or harassment. We could also add to this forms of organized conflict like strikes or protests. It is possible to see how widespread workplace conflict is from reports by organizations like ACAS (the Advisory, Conciliation and Arbitration Service – a non-governmental body that provides advice and mediates employment disputes) in the UK. These provide interesting insights into low-level or hidden conflict. As one report notes, 'almost all organizations experience disputes as part of their day-to-day activities' and they are 'challenging to precisely define since they take such a wide range of forms'.[3] ACAS has estimated that workplace conflict costs bosses £28.5 billion each year. This is around £1,000 for each worker per year, or just under £3,000 per year for each worker involved in a conflict. It is estimated that each year, 900,000 workers take time off because of conflict, 500,000 quit, and 300,000 are sacked.[4]

These statistics are a problem for bosses. They are evidence of trouble at work, and organizations like ACAS will often try to diagnose the problems and offer solutions. However, they do not ask why conflict is happening in the first place. In the previous chapters, we discussed the contradiction at the centre of work. However, there is no set rate of exploitation that all bosses choose to use. Instead, there is a kind of 'effort bargain' in which workers exchange their effort for the reward of pay. It is in the interests of bosses to shift the 'effort bargain' in their favour, while it is in workers' interests to pull in the other direction. In the boss's ideal world you would start work at full pace and work non-stop until the end of the day. You might even start before your official hours and maybe even work beyond your paid hours. This is not the reality that many of us have at work. We want to have a chat with people we work with. We have tea or coffee, take a smoke break, scroll on our phones in the bathroom. We want to act like people instead of machines.

Of course, there are other kinds of conflict that can emerge at work. These could be between workers or with customers in consumer-focused roles. It can tie in with oppression, too – for example, with a racist manager who is able to use their power at work to discriminate. Indeed, bosses may use racism, sexism and other forms of oppression to divide and rule, perhaps playing one group against another or trying to direct attention away from their own exploitation. The economic contradiction drives conflict again and again. Bosses are not content to let the 'effort bargain' stay the same. If workers can work a little harder, then why not try a bit more. New ways to manage or control workers get introduced. These may involve huge restructures or simply small changes.

The push from employers to change work is legitimated by the employment contract, and workers pushing back are seen as disrupting the workplace. The employment contract is about power between us and our bosses. If you leave work early, you will not get paid. But if you work longer than your shift, you may not get paid overtime. We rarely think about this as the employer stealing from workers, but that is what it is: wage theft. For example, in many kinds of work, the boss tells us we have to arrive 15 minutes before our shift. It is often justified as making sure we are prepared to start work when the shift begins. In the US, the Fair Labor Standards Act requires bosses to compensate workers for all the time they are at work. However, US judges have ruled that preparation time of less than ten minutes per day is *de minimis* and does not need to be paid. Imagine if you added up all those ten-minute slots each day for every worker having to do this. It would amount to a huge total. It makes sense why some white-collar workplaces have free food or showers on site – convincing workers to stay late is very profitable for bosses.

Wage Theft

We have organized with the IWGB in many workplaces where workers were not paid correctly. Dodgy payslips, vague deductions, missing hours and smaller paycheques are common across low-paid work. Stealing money from paycheques, like convincing workers to stay late, is a profitable practice. For example, there are estimates in the US that employers steal around $15 billion annually in minimum wage violations (around $3,300 per worker).[5] Previous estimates put overtime violations at $8.8 billion, rest break violations at $4 billion, and off-the-clock violations at $3.2 billion.[6] In the UK in 2020–2021, HMRC recovered £16 million in pay owed to 155,000 workers, as well as issuing £14 million in fines. And this is likely only scratching the surface of unpaid wages. HMRC released what they called the 'absurd excuses' that bosses have used for not paying the national minimum wage. They are revealing:

1. 'She does not deserve the National Minimum Wage because she only makes the teas and sweeps the floors.'
2. 'The employee was not a good worker, so I did not think they deserved to be paid the National Minimum Wage.'
3. 'My accountant and I speak a different language – he does not understand me, and that is why he does not pay my workers the correct wages.'
4. 'My employee is still learning so they are not entitled to the National Minimum Wage.'
5. 'It is part of UK culture not to pay young workers for the first three months as they have to prove their "worth" first.'
6. 'The National Minimum Wage does not apply to my business.'
7. 'I have got an agreement with my workers that I will not pay them the National Minimum Wage; they understand, and they even signed a contract to this effect.'
8. 'I thought it was okay to pay young workers below the National Minimum Wage as they are not British and therefore do not have the right to be paid it.'
9. 'My workers like to think of themselves as being self-employed and the National Minimum Wage does not apply to people who work for themselves.'

10. 'My workers are often just on standby when there are no customers in the shop; I only pay them for when they are actually serving someone.'[7]

These statements give a revealing picture of how some bosses justify wage theft, particularly given that this is what they were prepared to say during an investigation. Just imagine what they say behind closed doors. It is also worth noting that breaking the law, in this instance, is only paying below the legal minimum. In the UK, the minimum wage at the time of print is only £9.50 for those over 23, £9.18 for age 21–22, £6.83 for 18–20, £4.81 for those under 18 and £4.81 for apprentices. The government recently renamed this the 'National Living Wage' for workers over the age of 23 – however, it falls well below the living wage of £11.05 in London calculated by the independent Living Wage Foundation.[8] This means a huge number of people are getting less than what they need to have a reasonable standard of living. This is a huge theft from one class to enrich the other.

In the US, federal minimum wage is $7.25 per hour.[9] However, this only applies to 'covered' enterprises, including those involved in interstate commerce, with an annual volume of sales/business over $500,000, or work in healthcare, schools or government agencies. Workers who receive tips can have these counted towards the minimum wage, meaning an employer only has to pay $2.13 an hour in wages. Some states have higher minimum wages, including some that are more than double the federal level. Like in the UK, wage theft is a widespread feature of work in the US. For example, between 2017 and 2020, more than $3 billion in stolen wages was recovered by the US Department of Labor. This is also likely only the tip of the iceberg, as 'the vast majority of workers will never file a claim to recover stolen wages', perhaps as low as 2 per cent of those who could do so.[10] As one report explained:

> Even the theft of seemingly small amounts of time can have a large impact. Consider a full-time, minimum wage worker earning the federal minimum wage of $7.25 an hour who works just 15 minutes 'off the clock' before and after their shift every day. That extra half-hour of unpaid work each day represents a loss to the worker (and a gain to the employer) of around $1,400 per year, including the overtime premiums they should have been paid. That's nearly 10% of their annual earnings lost to their employer that can't be used for utilities, groceries, rent, or other necessities.[11]

This goes beyond the daily theft from workers under capitalism: getting paid less than we produce as workers. There is a very long history of making workers do more within the same time or extending the time of work. Marx, writing about factory work, described the process of 'these "small thefts" of capital from the labourer's meal and recreation time, the factory inspectors also designate as "petty pilferings of minutes", "snatching a few minutes", or, as the labourers technically called them, "nibbling and cribbling at meal-times" '. The push to make more and more time productive for the boss shows that 'moments are the elements of profit'.[12] The fight over the length of the lunch break, having paid overtime or even the correct pay matters.

Wage theft is one example of conflict in the workplace. The bosses on one side are trying to increase the profits they can make. Shifts change, targets increase, the workday gets extended, you have to put in more effort, and so on. In this context, resistance from workers can come in many forms. One of the most common is complaining with other workers who are experiencing the same thing. Think about the conversations you might have had during the work day, while out on a break or after work.

Resistance

Resistance at work can take many forms. It could be taking an extra-long lunch break, refusing to cooperate, making formal complaints, taking legal action, sabotage, theft or just leaving the job. Many of these are individual actions, but if there is one constant at work, it is that we find other people who share (at least some of) our experiences. Maybe we complain together about the worst parts of the work. We can share humour that only our co-workers would get about the job, celebrate the good parts or share tips and tricks to get by. Sometimes this can escalate into ways to try to avoid extra work or change the work to our benefit.

Many of these actions can make us feel better about a job,

providing a sort of pressure valve for the frustrations of going to work. Ignoring a request from a manager or complaining to another person can make work a bit more bearable. In a call centre that Jamie worked in, there was a worker who would break the headset cable at the start of a shift. This never stopped him from having to work. It did keep him off the phone at the start of the shift while the supervisor found a replacement. At the more extreme end, there are some heroic forms of individual resistance. For example, a building supervisor in Spain kept collecting his salary for six years without going into work. He spent his time reading philosophy instead. He was only discovered after, ironically, getting an award for twenty years of 'loyal service'.[13]

We often hear much more about lazy workers or slackers than we ever hear about wage theft. We might worry that if we get into conflict at work, the manager will give us a hard time or even threaten not to give a reference for the next job. However, if we never try to push back the frontier of control, it will keep moving in the bosses' favour.

One of the important parts of work is that it is, mostly, a collective experience. When we start to do things together to resist at work, we are able to make real change. One worker standing up to a boss risks retaliation. Many workers doing the same builds collective power. In most workplaces we can find collective forms of resistance. They are often quite hard to see from the outside. The problem with understanding – or even measuring – workplace conflict is that it is often hidden. When we look at 'official' measures of workplace conflict, we only get part of the story. Instead of looking at the figures of 'formal organisation', as George Rawick argued, we need

> the figures on how many ... hours were lost to production because of strikes, the amount of equipment and material destroyed by industrial sabotage and deliberate negligence, the amount of time lost by absenteeism, the hours gained by workers through the slowdown, the limiting of the speed-up of the productive apparatus through the working class's own initiative.[14]

As we discussed in the first part of the book, there are many different forms of resistance and workplace struggle. The classic example is the strike, which targets the core of the work relationship, the selling of our labour-power to an employer. The first ever recorded mass refusal of work was in ancient Egypt in 1170 BC. Artisans of the Royal Necropolis repeatedly refused work due to missing or late rations from the pharaoh, Ramesses III, and they won.[15] In 1768, sailors in London struck (lowered) their sails and joined a mass work stoppage, preventing commerce on the river Thames – and giving name to the strike.[16]

In the many years that have followed, we have won just about everything through either strikes or the threat of strikes. The definition of a strike is 'a temporary stoppage of work by a group of employees in order to express a grievance or enforce a demand'. Richard Hyman argues that each part of this is important for understanding strikes. First, the strike is 'temporary', as workers intend to return to work at the conclusion – and bosses normally view the dispute in the same way. Second, it involves 'stoppage of work', so it is distinct from actions like an overtime ban or go-slow. Third, it involves a 'group' of workers so it is a collective action. Fourth, it involves 'employees', meaning that workers strike, but other examples, like student strikes, are only strikes 'by analogy'. Finally, 'a strike is almost always a *calculative* act, designed to express a grievance or enforce a demand.'[17]

When we refuse work together, our jobs (hopefully) do not get done, and this has huge financial implications for bosses. Work simply cannot go on without workers, so the strike hits the boss in their pockets. It disrupts the economic process in the workplace. It often also involves the boss then refusing to pay workers. A strike is a standoff between the workers on one side and bosses on the other, vying to see who will surrender first. The picket line is a physical manifestation of this standoff. Pickets form a boundary at the entrance to the workplace to convince other workers not to cross. People who cross the picket line are called 'scabs'. The term comes from an Old English insult for a 'mean, low, "scurvy" fellow' but later became an insult for strikebreakers.[18] By choosing to break a strike, scabs undermine the collective power of workers.

The strike and the picket line are the most visible examples of workplace conflict, but there are many other forms of workplace struggle that can be powerful. For example, 'work to rule'. This involves only carrying out the work that is specified in our contracts. Often our employment contracts do not match with what we do every day at work. The reality is that we often do much more. Think of jobs that you have worked; often, much of the work is not clearly defined. Similarly, if we follow every requirement in our contract to the letter, we can slow down the work. Sometimes our contract asks us to follow rules that are contradictory in practice. This can prevent work from carrying on. Rather than breaking the rules, sometimes just following them can cause disruption.

In the UK, this is what's called 'action short of strike' (ASOS), which has been used by university workers as part of their industrial action in the UK.[19] Other forms of ASOS include go-slows (work that is deliberately slowed), overtime bans (a refusal to do overtime) or callout bans (a refusal to work outside of contracted hours). Workers have also found more creative ways to disrupt their work. For example, bus drivers in Sydney refused to take fares for a day in protest. The 'fare-free day' meant they carried on driving the buses, but people using the service did not have to pay.[20] In another example, Cathay Pacific cabin crew engaged in a 'smile strike'. They refused to deliver on their usual 'service with a smile' – as well as threatening not to serve drinks or food. They also proposed work to rule with complex airline regulations. This meant risking expensive delays on flights taking off.[21]

The unique aspects of each workplace bring new challenges and opportunities for action. In some cases, like health, care or education, workers may want to disrupt in ways that affect the boss and not people they work with. For example, in the 1970 postal strike in the US, workers promised to deliver welfare checks even while they were striking.[22]

There is also a long history of sabotage in the labour movement (though it has often been condemned by those wanting to be respectable). Big Bill Haywood, the Industrial Workers of the World (IWW) leader, gave a speech in 1911 in which he said: 'I don't know of anything that can be applied that will bring as much satisfaction to you, as much anger to the boss as a little sabotage in the right place at the right time. Find out what it means. It won't hurt you and it will cripple the boss.'[23] Sabotage involves disrupting the work process. This can mean finding creative ways to slow things down, not looking after equipment or generally trying to frustrate the boss.[24]

Beyond sabotage and strikes there is another tactic worth noting: occupying the workplace. There are instances in which workers will not only picket outside. Instead they take over the workplace and prevent its operation. They can even continue its operation with self-management. For example, after the owners of the VIO.ME soap factory in Greece filed for bankruptcy in 2011, workers occupied the factory. Since then, they have been cooperatively running the factory, distributing the tasks and profits among themselves. They have since moved to producing ecological soap and were able to distribute it through solidarity networks during the pandemic.[25]

There are then forms of action that take place outside of the workplace that can be effective at pressuring the boss inside the workplace. Outside the workplace a company or organization's reputation can be key to its functioning and profit making. Damaging, or threatening to damage, reputations can give workers a lot of leverage. This can involve appealing to the media and the public or through boycotts. For example, during the strikes at Deliveroo in 2016 in the UK, social media was used to spotlight the conditions of the work – while also raising almost £13,000 to support the strike.[26] In other cases, universities have been publicly shamed as part of a national media campaign organized by cleaners, damaging their reputation and making student recruitment harder.

Resistance can also come through use of the law. Labour or employment tribunals are not often friends of workers. On their own, this tactic can be expensive and individualizing. But the law can be weaponised as part of a wider workplace struggle, another way to turn up the heat, and there are plenty of examples of workers winning significant financial payouts.

There will always be resistance at work. Whether it takes the small forms of grumbling or gossip, individual actions, legal fights or huge collective struggles, it is always there. It is important to start from the workplace and consider what forms of resistance already exist before trying to think about what kind of resistance or organization could be effective. Otherwise, we risk thinking of only the official statistics or institutions, missing the wider picture of class struggle.

9
TRADE UNIONISM

Organizing at work starts with relationships between workers. It means building networks and preparing to take action together. It is from these networks that workers have built longer-term forms of organization, trade unions being one of these forms. Unions, at their heart, are collective organizations of workers. The first trade unions in the UK formed in the seventeenth century. During the industrial revolution, there were waves of struggle over working conditions and from these, workers started local trade unions.

The establishment of unions was a victory in itself. Bosses initially refused to negotiate and used all the power available to them to fight unions; they were not afraid to use the force of the state, thugs and even the military to try to stop worker organizing. In rural England, six men were convicted of swearing a secret oath as members of the Friendly Society of Agricultural Labourers in 1834. They were sentenced to penal transportation to Australia. These men became known as the Tolpuddle Martyrs. Their cause was taken up by supporters across England, who gathered 800,000 signatures and organized a protest march of up to 100,000 people in London. This was no easy feat before the invention of e-petitions and social media. Campaigners collected signatures and support by going door-to-door and hosting local meetings. They were eventually pardoned and became an important symbol of resistance in labour movement history. They are remembered with both a museum and an annual Tolpuddle Martyrs' Festival.[1]

In the US, during the Coal Wars of the nineteenth century, coal companies fought unions tooth and nail, using private detectives, law enforcement and hired enforcers to prevent union organizing. In West Virginia, companies met an organizing drive by the United Mine Workers of America with violence. They sought to forcibly evict union members from company towns, and the confrontations led to a shootout with the Baldwin-Felts Detective Agency in Matewan in 1920. The 'Matewan Massacre', as it became known, became a rallying point for miners struggling for a union. A year later, the US army crushed a demonstration of 7,000 striking miners. The Battle of Blair Mountain lasted five days; during that time, a million rounds of ammunition were fired, the Air Corps used bombers and as many as a hundred strikers were killed.[2] The result of the battle was a major setback for unionizing the West Virginia coalfields.

Even the process of setting up unions has historically been met with hostility and violence from the bosses. This can be easy to forget today, yet the fact that there is an entire industry that has been established to stop you and your co-workers from organizing shows that the bosses are still scared of workers' power. In 2019 Delta Airlines put up posters explaining that 'Union dues cost around $700 [£580] a year . . . A new video game system with the latest hits sounds like fun. Put your money towards that instead of paying dues to the union.'[3] Whole Foods (owned by Amazon) developed a system with at least twenty-four metrics to develop a heat map to track potential unionization.[4] Companies like Perceptyx offer specialised forms of 'predictive analytics in HR' that firms can purchase to counteract 'vulnerability to union organizing'.[5]

They may have the money, resources, media, consultants and new technologies, but we have the one thing that they do not have: we make capitalism function. Without us, they do not make money. It is that simple. To effectively use the power we possess, we need to find a way to connect across different workplaces. We need to understand how to associate strikes by cleaners with those of bus drivers, utility workers and office workers on the other side of the country. Currently, what unites us is abstract. We do not know each other, we do not understand each other's issues, nor do we act in unison. Unions are an important starting point for building that latent power.

The main aim of unions is to get a better deal out of the selling of labour-power. When we go to work we start as individuals, and the balance of power is firmly in the hands of the bosses: they own the means of production and can choose who to hire. We may not know much about the conditions of work before starting.

Unions provide an organizational way to shift that power balance. We go from being isolated workers to collective bodies that can bargain against bosses. Worker organizing through trade unions has transformed conditions of work. We have achieved huge gains through organizing together. Higher wages, weekends, paid holidays, paid family leave, more security and stability, health and safety protections, protection against discrimination, legal support and better terms and conditions. It should therefore be no wonder that bosses have opposed them.

Unions are mass organizations. This means that they have a broad membership – members get signed up based on where they work, rather than on shared politics or perspectives. Members pay fees to join the union, often on a subscription basis – paying 'subs'. This money is then pooled and, in theory, spent on furthering worker's interests. Unions rely on member subs to operate, so (also in theory) this means they have to fight in the interests of the majority of workers if they want to keep functioning.

Unions may operate in a single workplace, sector, industry or across a country. Some unions are for a specific kind of occupation. Others have grown into large, amalgamated unions where smaller unions have merged to form general unions. Protecting the interests of workers is the main function of unions, but this can involve many types of activities. Broadly, the main activity of unions is bargaining at work and negotiating settlements. Depending on the context, this can mean binding agreements or signing a contract to end a dispute, collective bargaining or dealing with smaller issues. They can negotiate with a single employer or organize strikes across whole sectors. Many also engage in 'casework', which is the bread and butter of worker organizing. It involves dealing with issues that members are having with their bosses, from unpaid wages to an issue with the contract, a bullying manager, harassment or any number of other problems that can happen at work. Union functions have grown over time, with many also providing training and education. They might build solidarity between members and with other causes and campaigns. Or they might try to find ways to exert political influence beyond the workplace.

Like with all mass organizing, ideology and values are important. Collective action is not radical in and of itself. Reactionary or oppressive ideas can drive action too. For example, police unions in the US use their power to prevent justice, protecting racist and corrupt cops. Due to the role of police in protecting the interests of the powerful, most do not consider police unions part of the workers' movement. On the other hand, the Chicago Teachers Union demanded a progressive agenda beyond the workplace in their 2019 campaign. They included a demand for affordable housing in the city for students and teachers as part of their strike. This involved using their leverage and power to bring more to the bargaining table – not only pay and benefits, but more radical changes in the community. It was part of a wider movement in the US of 'bargaining for the common good'.[6] This involves building long-term community labour-power to tackle structural issues like racial injustice.

It can be quite difficult to talk about unions in general terms. As they are democratic organizations, unions operate in different ways in practice. They are shaped by the traditions and histories of the sector or industry they operate in. National or regional legal requirements can change how they work. Not all unions have stuck to their core union functions, either. In many European countries, the union movement is divided into politically aligned federations. For example, there are unions with communist history, socialist, Christian or even conservative politics. There is also the IWW or the 'Wobblies', a form of revolutionary industrial unionism that emphasises workplace democracy and the power of members. You also might find 'yellow unions' that are captured by the boss or are no longer independent. The largest union in the world, the All-China Federation of Trade Unions (ACFTU) has an estimated 300 million members – and a million full-time officials – but is not independent from the state. The grassroots enterprise unions that make up the foundation of the union 'are largely under the control of the enterprise management'. It is illegal for workers to form a union outside of this structure.[7]

While unions come in all shapes and sizes, there are distinctions that are useful to make. There are, broadly speaking, four kinds of unions. First, craft unions. These organize with workers based on the skill involved or the kind of work they do – for example, carpenters being part of a woodworkers' union. Craft unions may organize workers across different industries but tend to be smaller and concerned with setting boundaries around who can do their kind of work. Controlling this can be part of developing bargaining power. It also means they might work alongside workers who are not eligible to join the same union. Second, industrial unions organize with workers across one industry, regardless of the level or job of the worker. The strength of this model comes from the ability to strike to shut down the whole supply chain. The IWW is one example of radical industrial unionism. While they accept all members, they focus on organizing whole industries, like factories, mining, utilities and transportation. Third, professional unions are like craft unions, but they have grown in so-called white-collar professions. For example, academic workers in the UCU (University and College Union) in the UK is only open to academic or academic-related workers in universities and colleges, not to the wider workforce. Fourth are the general unions that recruit workers from any industry or sector. Most unions today are closer to this kind of model, and many of them are the result of mergers. For example, the SEIU (Service Employees International Union) in the US or Unite in the UK. These unions can grow to be very large, with many having membership in the millions. They may have a blend of craft, professional and industrial unionism within them, depending on their history.

We also distinguish unions by the model they use. While all unions need to do some of the core union functions (membership administration, accounting, running a website, and so on) they differ greatly in what they spend the rest of their annual budgets on. There are two broad union models. There is the servicing or business model, which focuses on servicing members' individual needs. It treats members like consumers, and the union is a business. Members have 'needs' and the union can address them, typically through casework (most often) or negotiating on their behalf. The union will have a clear hierarchy with specialised paid staff who take on roles and who form what is thought of as 'the union'. There is little place for democratic debate or discussion, and members consider themselves getting something from the union, not *being* the union. Instead, decisions are left to 'professionals' hired by the union, who then speak for members. As Kim Moody has argued, 'business unionism as an outlook is fundamentally conservative in that it leaves unquestioned capital's dominance, both on the job and in society as a whole. Instead, it seeks only to negotiate the price of this domination'.[8] In the US, some service unions even go as far as to agree to non-strike clauses in contracts with employers. It can also entail entering into partnerships with the employer, undermining the independence of the union.

The second is the organizing model. In contrast with the servicing/business model, it focuses on how members of a union can 'organize'. This can mean many things, including recruiting members, building their confidence and fighting campaigns. This often, still, relies on paid organizers who are external to the workforce.[9] Unlike the servicing model, though, it does try to build the power of workers within the workplace and the union. There are, of course, disagreements about what organizing should involve – or what we are organizing for.[10] In some cases, this has meant the development of new kinds of unionism, like community unionism, which tries to engage communities beyond the labour movement in struggles through, for example, churches or other faith-based organizations. There is also social movement unionism. For this, the union organizes around broader struggles than just economic, including social justice. There are also more radical forms of syndicalism, like that found with the IWW. These forms emphasise the self-activity of workers in unions. They are generally opposed to the use of paid union officials or other forms of bureaucracy.

As a socialist, you may want to be in a revolutionary union. There is a history of setting up revolutionary unions, although this tactic has not proven that successful. This can lead to the most radical workers splitting from the rest. For example, in the UK, the EPIU (Electrical and Plumbing Industries Union) broke away from the EETPU (Electrical, Electronic, Telecommunications and Plumbing Union). This took a minority of militant workers away from the larger membership of the EETPU and created two problems. First, bosses refused to negotiate with the EPIU, choosing the other union instead. Second, the right-wing leadership was no longer challenged in the EETPU. This does not mean that there are not cases where the establishment of new unions is a good idea. For example, UVW and IWGB both started as part of a larger union. Latin American cleaners formed these unions in response to being locked out of union democracy in larger unions and needing a union that operated in their language. They organized in Spanish, to include all workers in their workplaces, and made sure every cleaner had access to legal help in their own language. This is not the same dynamic as breaking away a militant core. Instead, they built unions that represented the majority of workers in the workplaces they operated in, something their original union was incapable of. Separating also allowed experiments in tactics and strategies that would not otherwise have been possible.

While there are more radical forms of unions, the core activity of unions is not. Bargaining is not about overthrowing capitalism or transforming society. As Marx pointed out: 'unions work well as centres of resistance against the encroachments of capital.' However, they are limited 'to a guerrilla war against the effects of the existing system, instead of simultaneously trying to change it'.[11] Unions focus on getting workers a better deal under capitalism. We must, however, get involved in unions in our fight for much more than that.

Any socialist worth their salt should get involved with worker organizing. Unions are mass organizations involved in the day-to-day fight against capitalism. Whether in bigger or newer organizations, unions are a vital part of the workers' movement. Engels argued that 'as schools of war, the Unions are unexcelled'.[12] They provide anti-capitalist training in two ways. First, they are a vehicle to push back against exploitation and control at work, providing practical tools for building power and giving a glimpse of what workers' power could look like. Second, unions are democratic bodies of workers. They are a place to come together to debate and take action. While unions may not be revolutionary in their day-to-day activity, what happens within them can hold the key to unlocking a new future.

Unions began as a way to fight the boss. As unions become larger, they get more remote from that workplace fight. What happens in one workplace starts to become less important. Developing structures and resources allows unions to keep operating between strikes and campaigns, as well as fighting beyond one workplace. In the process, union bureaucracies can also begin to develop their own interests. We can see this with massive unions like SEIU in the US or Unite in the UK. They have more than a million members and budgets in the millions. In an organization of this size, it should be no surprise that staff may start to worry about maintaining the union as an institution rather than one worker campaign or another. Diverging interests can then emerge between the union and the rank and file of the membership.

The Bureaucracy and Rank and File

A bureaucracy is a social layer of people – bureaucrats – who work for an organisation. The role of bureaucrats is to administer the organization. In a union, the bureaucracy is the paid staff, but it can also mean elected officials, particularly if they spend time away from the workplace. This includes the membership administrators, finance managers, caseworkers, organizers, the general secretary and the president. As they do not work alongside members, bureaucrats are removed from the experience of the workplace. They are not subject to the same day-to-day pressures, and victories or losses do not have the same material effect on them. For example, staff and officials' wages depend on the continuation of the union, while members' wages can depend on taking serious (and militant) action. Members might want to walk off the job without balloting for a strike. This can be a powerful tool to fight the boss by catching them off guard. However, in the UK, this could lead to expensive fines and legal injunctions against the union. While militant action might be in the members' interest, it would not be in the interest of staff and officials. Though not always the case, these material interests may mean bureaucrats have a tendency to be more conservative.

There are some obvious risks as bureaucracies develop. First, creating specialised union staff or officials involves a division of labour. Staff develop specific expertise that separate them from the membership, professionalizing union activities. This can make it hard for us to do tasks ourselves, consigning us to watch from the bench while tasks are done for us. Second, it can undermine the democracy of a union. The interests of the bureaucracy can lead to different tactics and strategies. These are often less radical and are less likely to get us a win.

The classic example is asking the bureaucracy for a strike ballot. They are hesitant about calling a strike ballot, because it could damage their relationship with the boss, with whom they are used to negotiating. There could be reluctance to let you use union resources. If they have not spent time talking with workers, they have not seen the energy for taking action. It becomes an abstract debate. The hesitancy of the bureaucracy then disempowers workers and prevents action. It can become another hurdle during a campaign and unfortunately is very common in the UK.

We have both experienced many examples of the dragging dynamic of bureaucracy on worker militancy in practice. At a meeting of excited, and in some cases new, workers of a big union, the starting time for the meeting came and went. The union staffer who usually ran the meeting did not turn up. None of the workers had ever run a union meeting before, as the staffer always did it. There was a reluctance to start without the authority of the staffer. They were so used to having a professional organizer that it had disempowered them from running their own meetings. This was the very organization that was meant to be building their power.

In a separate instance, one staffer in a big union claimed there were two groups of people present in the union meeting (over casualization in a university): one group that wanted to go on strike and others who wanted a resolution. They appealed to those who wanted to strike not to disrupt the negotiation process and to leave it in their safe hands as professional negotiators to bargain with the bosses. The staffer valued their relationship with management more than with the members and saw striking as an unnecessary disruption to this. This meant even going as far as to attack members who wanted to go on strike. Across the labour movement there are countless examples of this: the strike that was shut down or sold out, the blocking of a motion or decision by staff.

Union bureaucracy is a product of social relations under capitalism. The problems this can create are not the result of the personal deficiencies of bureaucrats, but come from the different material interests. They sit between workers and the boss, subject to pressure from both. On the one hand, they have 'pressure from above'. This includes the bosses and all their 'institutions – political and non-political, state and non-state'. If this pressure from above wins out, unions can be an important channel for bosses to influence and control workers. Based on these negative experiences, it might sound reasonable to be against bureaucracy. Maybe we should try and do away with it. However, the fact is that if we want to build mass organizations, we need it. We were part of a union that grew from 1,000 to more than 6,000 members. As it grew, there were new demands on the organization. It began to need dedicated staff to function – for example, to maintain a finance system for subs, a database for membership and a licence to represent workers in court. It is simply not feasible to have some of a large organization's administrative functions done in someone's spare time. These roles can also free up lay members to organize at work.

Given the existence of bureaucracy inside of unions, the key issue is what we should do about it. There are four possibilities. First, we do nothing. Second, we leave big bureaucratised unions and do something different. This might work for a time, until the new organization gets bigger and develops its own bureaucracy. Third, we seek to replace the 'bad' bureaucrats with 'good' ones.

The workers' movement is full of interesting personalities and characters, many of whom have led incredible struggles. While a strong character can push back on some of the pressures, no matter how good they are, they will come under the pressures we have discussed. Over time, they will spend less time doing the things that made them 'good' in the first place. The most effective worker-leaders are forged through collective struggles. It is through these that people learn the skills and the confidence to become effective. Election to positions and taking on roles in the union removes leaders from the very conditions that made them so effective.

No individual, no matter how talented or charismatic they are, can solve the structural problems of union bureaucracy. Instead, we must develop a rank-and-file approach to organizing in unions. If bosses can create pressure on the union bureaucracy from above, we can apply 'pressure from below'. This is the contradiction of union leadership, and it is determined through these pressures. If we do not provide a counterbalancing force on the bureaucracy, it should be no surprise that they will react to the pressure applied 'from above'.[13]

The rank and file is the membership of the union. It includes workers who pay their subs to the union but are not elected to leadership or officer positions. This also, of course, excludes paid union staff. Ray, an experienced rank-and-file organizer in Scotland, explains what the strategy involves. He argues that in unions, 'the key division between left and right' is 'less important than the divisions between rank-and-file and bureaucracy'.[14] This might not be in tune with experiences that we have had in unions. Maybe we have found some other left-wing members, officials or staffers to talk to about organizing. If you have spent any time organizing in a union, you will have likely come across right-wingers, too. If we identify with the left, it might make sense to seek out others who share our politics. As Ray argues, this is not the point of a rank-and-file strategy. It aims to build up the capacity, consciousness and combativity of the membership. This means building pressure 'from below' and aiming to force the union bureaucracy into acting, while also creating the possibility to act without them. Ray's point is not that the difference between the left and right is not important. It will involve, of course, challenging right-wing ideas and oppression that we come across. The point is that even if they identify as 'right', workers have more in common with each other than they do with bureaucrats who might agree with them otherwise.

It can be very difficult to find practical examples of a rank-and-file approach today, as there have been many years without a confident rank and file in many unions. We can look back to moments in the 1930s in the US or later.[15] Arguably, the last high point in the UK and the US was the end of the 1970s,[16] but much has changed since then. As Hal Draper has argued, in practice, 'one encounters a tremendous amount of variation'.[17] What the rank and file looks like will change with context, whether in relation to the kind of work, sector of the economy or the current political moment. The return of interest in rank-and-file politics, seen with both the renewed popularity of *Labor Notes* in the US[18] and *Strike Map* in the UK,[19] is to be welcomed. We then need to try to find ways to build rank-and-file power in our new contexts.

Organizing Today

Across the chapters in this part of the book, we have discussed a range of ideas about work. We started by trying to understand what work is under capitalism. It is common today to hear people say that work has changed. Clearly, work has been transformed since the start of capitalism; however, the core relationship between bosses and workers is still there. This means that we can learn from past workers' struggles. Looking at previous tactics and strategies can inform our actions today.

The main challenge is translating these lessons from the past or other struggles into today. By starting with the concepts put forward in the previous chapters, we can think through the issues in ways that draw attention to the actual struggles of workers. However, we need to do more than just think about these issues. The key to these ideas is putting them into practice by trying to organize.

The first issue that you will face in organizing is confidence. When you first start trying to organize, people will say: 'it's not possible' or 'they/we are unorganizable'. And you might feel this yourself. However, as discussed throughout the first part of this book, there are no 'unorganizable' workers or any sector where organizing cannot work. There is no 'unorganizable' – just 'yet-to-get-organized'. This idea of workers being 'unorganizable' often comes from the very people whose job title may be 'organizer': Lydia was once told by a regional union official responsible for organizing cleaners at the university that they could not be organized because they were too divided along lines of nationality to ever come together. Two years later, those same cleaners went on to lead a fierce and disruptive majority strike that ended outsourcing at the London School of Economics. Unsurprisingly, they had joined a different union.

Partly as a result of ideas like this, there are many industries yet to be organized, and many unions have not taken organizing with migrant and precarious workers seriously. However, there is another commonly held belief that holds back organizing, and it is the flip side of the previous one: that workers are too comfortable to organize. This can leave us in a strange position of having some workers too precarious and the others not being precarious enough. Whichever way you turn, someone will try to find a 'reason' why organizing is not possible. If there is one constant in organizing, it is that you will meet many people who feel this deeply. Some of the most common objections are that workers in the industry are too right wing, isolated or just not interested. There may not be a clear workplace — no factory gates at which to speak to people. Worker turnover might be high, with workers not staying long enough to get organized. The kind of work might be different or unusual, giving the impression that organizing cannot work. This line of thinking is so common that every single group of workers we have met has said something similar.

It should come as no surprise that this is a common feeling: organizing is hard and we have had anti-union and anti-organizing ideas pushed on us for a very long time by mainstream media and government. But it has been done — and it can be done *anywhere*. This is not to say there is a one-size-fits-all model, nor that it will be easy. We can learn from previous struggles, but if the old tactics do not work, then we will need to create new ones.

III
THE ART OF
TROUBLEMAKING

10

WORKERS' INQUIRIES

Work is still a problem. We may not think that our individual job is important, but together with other workers, it forms part of the overall capitalist system. Our work is one part in a huge jigsaw. By having to do it every day, each of us becomes experts in how our workplace and industry functions. Our own individual experiences may not offer much insight into how capitalism works, but when combined with others we can start to see a much bigger picture. By building that picture for ourselves, we can understand capitalism today. We can see how it works and how it is changing. More importantly, we can see its relative strengths, weaknesses and vulnerabilities.

The problem is that we rarely get the opportunity to share our experiences. If we want to reorganize society, we need to develop an understanding of where we currently are. This needs to happen before we figure out where we want to be, let alone how we are going to get there. The beginnings of that understanding are out there already, it is just a matter of making those connections. Through shared struggles, we can start building a perspective that brings each of these pieces together.

This understanding is something that you might expect to be central to the left. Yet in many debates, questions about work or workers' organization are notably absent. Later in Marx's life, he published a survey in a French newspaper. He asked workers to respond to questions about the conditions of their work.[1] In his brief call for a workers' inquiry, Marx explained that workers 'alone can describe with full knowledge the misfortunes from which they suffer and that only they, and not saviors sent by providence, can energetically apply the healing remedies for the social ills which they are prey'.[2] This sets out an important principle. If we want to understand struggles at work, we as workers are the only people capable of documenting them. More than that, we are the only force capable of winning a struggle to transform our world.

This is the idea of a workers' inquiry. It is a method that combines research with organizing. It is a process of discovery, not only of the conditions of work now but also how to fight them. Workers' inquiries can involve the postal survey that Marx tried or more collaborative methods like interviewing, co-writing, worker writing, discussions and more. There is a long history of political groups using workers' inquiries – for example, the Johnson–Forest Tendency in the US, Socialisme ou Barbarie in France and the Italian Operaismo or Workerists.[3] Each group was trying to understand how work had changed and the implication this had for how we organize.

In our current moment, workers' inquiries can play an important role. In the first part of the book, we discussed a range of struggles at work. Throughout each, you can see important moments that tell us something about what is possible. However, we can also learn something important from our work. The reason we are introducing the idea of workers' inquiries is to provide a method of both thinking about and taking action at work. We cannot exactly replicate previous struggles in our own workplaces, but we can find inspiration.

Workers' inquiries do not start with any answers. We have each wished for a secret manuscript to be found in a dusty corner of an attic that gives us the recipe for making socialism. But, alas, no such thing exists. Instead we must build it ourselves for the twenty-first century. Inquiry provides a way to start asking the right questions about our work and organizing to get there. This also means starting with the people actually in the workplace – we need to understand that 'our experiences of work matter'.[4] Every struggle has to start by trying to understand the current conditions and how to change them. Workers' inquiries make this process explicit.

The kind of work we do, who we work with and the conditions under which we do it matter. In a recent collection of workers' inquiries, *From the Workplace*,[5] we shared the following guiding questions for writers who contributed to the collection to get started:

1. What do you do at work?
2. Who do you work with?
3. Who does your work affect? (Both inside and beyond your workplace.)
4. Who makes money from your work?
5. What leverage do you have at work?

These five questions provide a way to start exploring something called 'class composition'.

Class composition was an idea introduced by Italian Workerists to make sense of the workers' inquiries. This starts with the understanding of class as a relationship, as we have discussed in previous chapters. Classes are not abstract but are formed through struggles with each other. In practice, this is not a uniform process. It is messy, complicated and contradictory. Class composition is a way of unpicking the relationship of class by starting at the workplace.

In *Notes from Below*, we use class composition to analyse workers' inquiries by examining three parts. First is what is called 'technical composition'. This includes the factors related to work that we have discussed so far – it is the organization of labour-power by the boss in the workplace. This is the work actually carried out and the context within which it takes place. It includes things like technology, supervisors, techniques like Taylorism and all the other ways that management attempts to control workers. The second is 'social composition'. This is what life is like outside of the workplace. It is clear that the organization of work is important, but our conditions outside of work matter, too. This includes things like where we live, our communities, our social reproduction and treatment in society. It covers our relationship to the state with social services, migration, borders, policing, and so on.[6]

The reason for examining technical and social composition is to understand the crucial third part: 'political composition'. These are the tactics and strategies that we use to change our work, whether through strikes, protests or other kinds of collective solidarity. It also includes which types of organizations we create, whether networks, unions or political parties. The technical and social composition shape the forms of political composition that are possible. This is not a strict relationship, but when we look at historical examples, we can clearly see how the two are related.

For example, think of how the industrial revolution created specific kinds of technical and social compositions for workers. Many people moved from the countryside to work in factories in expanding cities. Their previous way of life was upturned, and they then worked very long hours inside large workplaces alongside many other workers. The conditions in the factory brought people together with shared interests in a way that had not existed before. The cramped living conditions near the factories helped to forge new communities. These new technical and social compositions combined to facilitate spontaneous forms of worker struggle that then grew into associations and early unions. The development of mass production in factories changed the technical composition of the work. Workers fought the assembly line in factories with strikes and slowdowns. They formed industrial unions that built power on the factory floor.

Since then, there have been many other examples of how class composition has changed. Either new compositions emerge or workers are decomposed. For example, the struggles of miners in both the UK and the US were shaped by the conditions in mines and the villages and towns that grew around them. This supported extended periods of strikes in which the wider community was important. However, the closure of mines and the moving of industry elsewhere effectively decomposed these communities, seen with the closure of pits in the UK and the rust belt in the US.

We know too little about how class composition is changing today. Take service work, for example. These jobs can be very different from either manufacturing or the public sector, often with small workplaces and no existing unions. The forms of organizing factory workers use will probably not be directly applicable and, in truth, we do not really know what is effective yet. Instead, we must find the new weak points for the boss while identifying our own strengths. This is why class composition is useful. It provides a way of thinking about the parts of our work and communities that may shape our struggles.

Class composition is a material relationship. It is about how class gets formed in both the workplace and society. However, it is both a product and a producer of struggle, as well as constantly changing through that struggle. It is also not only of interest to our side (although the bosses do not talk about it in these terms, of course); on the other side, bosses try to decompose workers. They well know how changing the technical composition at work impacts the political composition. Why do you think Amazon designs their fulfilment centres to isolate workers and prevent forming bonds of solidarity? This is about trying to stop workers from fighting back effectively. We can see this in the classic example of the boss threatening to automate work. Bosses recognise the risk of workers finding new and effective ways to struggle. But instead of taking them head on, they choose to change the technical composition – introducing, for example, new techniques, breakup processes, bring in machines, and so on. This is an attempt to decompose our power.

We can only find out where our power is by testing our ideas. This means building the knowledge we need ourselves. We are not suggesting that individuals need to come up with all these answers, but we each already possess knowledge that is important in forming the next steps. Each of us has an understanding of our work, and we are all experts in our own fragment of capitalism. What is it that we actually spend so much of our time doing? And most importantly, how can it be changed? We need to become experts in piecing these fragments together.

Most importantly, this is not about knowledge for knowledge's sake. It is about testing ideas in practice. In short, organizing. When we go to work, we are shaped by our work – our personalities, our ambitions, our view of the world, of people, and even our physical body. As Marx argued, it is not the consciousness of people that determines their existence, 'but their social existence that determines their consciousness'.[7] The way our lives are organized shapes our understanding. Our ideas change through engagement with the world – but by changing the world, we also become changed.

There is no comparison between the experience of debating ideas with someone and going through collective struggle together. No matter how many times someone tells us that we can organize and win, the experience of beating a boss is the only true way we can know it is possible. In chapter 1, Alex's experience organizing at TDL involved this shift clearly. His co-workers described the process as their own 'red pill' movement. Although this term has been seized upon by the far-right, they used it to describe their own moment of being like Neo in *The Matrix*: once they had won and seen it was possible, there was no going back.

There are few opportunities for us to genuinely have a say in how our lives are organized under capitalism. However, any victory, no matter how small, demonstrates where much more is possible, what our own power can achieve and it is a huge boost in our confidence. When we are confident, conscious and combative, as a movement and as individuals, anything is attainable. Confident workers demand more and fight harder, and they inspire others to try the same. The LSE cleaners from chapter 2 motivated cleaners at St Mary's with their victory against outsourcing. Beverly and Mildred, two of the LSE cleaners' most active voices, have visited countless picket lines across London and toured other workplaces encouraging cleaners to get active. Beverley in 2020 said to a room full of fellow union members, 'We just need the strength, the help and the support from each other; with that we can continue to fight for dignity, respect and equality'. They post almost daily in their union WhatsApp group words of encouragement to share with others. Building these links and connections is the other key to building what comes next.

We also need to think about how our activity connects the big to the small. The details of our work and organizing in a particular workplace are key to building the power we need to take on big political questions like the democratization of our lives and society, different ways of running the world, alternatives to climate apocalypse and the need for revolutionary change to get rid of capitalism. Too often, people are engaged in either the big or the small. Some spend their time discussing electoral or policy strategies, completely disconnected from the day-to-day struggles. Similarly, those involved in building power in smaller struggles get lost in the details, no longer seeing the bigger picture. We cannot debate our way out of capitalism, nor can we only fight at the micro level.

In the next chapters of the book, we discuss three workplace organizing principles that we believe can get us closer to doing this: the need for action, building the rank and file, and why democracy matters. We need to find ways to connect the big questions to our struggles in the workplace, as the smaller struggles are the building blocks from which we can develop the power necessary to make the big changes we want. This starts by investigating our own work. As Ed Emery put it: 'no politics without inquiry.'[8]

11
ACTION

During the writing of this book we were discussing with a friend his first experience of organizing. He was feeling a bit disheartened and wanted some advice. He and his co-workers had come together and written a letter to their boss. They wanted the boss to honour their commitment to no weekend working on the set of a television production. They provided a vital role on set as camera support equipment technicians (as grips) but were exhausted at the end of a week. Within hours, the producer got back to them saying simply, 'no'. The production needed to keep to schedule and they just had to get over it, apparently. This was a deflating experience that left them feeling like collective action could not work. When we read the letter they sent it became clear why it did not get the desired effect. There was no threat. The production company would face no consequences if they kept scheduling them to work weekends, other than a bit of awkwardness from knowingly asking employees to do something they do not want to do. When facing the toss-up between delaying a costly production by ending weekend work and a few disgruntled workers who sent a polite letter, it is clear what the producer would choose – and they did so.

This is why taking action is important. We do not win when we do not use our power, and taking action is how we reveal what power we have. It is how we gain confidence and how we can apply pressure on the boss. It is how we win and how we win big. Coming back to the principle we discussed from Jason Moyer-Lee in chapter 3, to win a campaign we need to make it more costly for the decision maker to maintain the status quo than it is for them to change it in our favour. The film workers could have threatened and planned a walkout on key strategic days in filming – for example, picking the only two days an expensive actor has to film their scenes. Then, removing weekend work all of a sudden becomes less expensive than dealing with a walkout which would mean rebooking an actor and extending filming to suit their schedule. Of course, that might have been quite a leap for a first threat of action, bearing in mind that a threat should never be empty and slower escalation can build your power. But the principle holds.

So, what action can we take? Well, the most discussed strategy is the strike. This is our most powerful tool, the mass refusal of workers to work. As Richard Hyman argues, a strike is a 'calculative' act,[1] and when it is in our favour, the power relationships of the workplace can be reversed. You may start doing that calculation in your own workplace: what if you and your co-workers stopped working, would it really matter that much? If you find yourself reaching the conclusion that it would not, do not worry. Many campaigns have been won by workers who felt similarly. Strike action can be combined with many other methods to make bosses feel the implications of not giving you what you want. For example, during the cleaner's campaign at St Mary's, the bosses tried to ship in workers to replace them, so much of their work was getting done. The cleaners thus combined the strikes with loud and disruptive protests. They shamed their employer in the press. They encouraged doctors from the workplace to speak out about their treatment.

It might also be that you think striking simply is not an option in your line of work. For example, you might be a care worker or do a role that has people other than your boss relying on you. While strikes can be incredibly powerful, there are also many other types of action we can take. When choosing what action to take, we need to come back to that basic equation of how to hit the boss financially. This might mean refusing to do parts of your job, educating clients or devising some other way to take action depending on the sector and the industry. This is also an example of how thinking about your own work can be important for organizing. Doing your own workers' inquiry and collectively exploring where your power lies is the first step. You as a worker in the industry are best equipped to figure out the most effective tactic.

All forms of industrial action are aimed at reducing productivity, disrupting the ability of the boss to make money or to run their service effectively. The most commonly used tools at our disposal beyond the strike are: go-slows (slowing down how productive we are), work to rule (only doing tasks required in our contracts), overtime bans (refusing to do any overtime, paid or unpaid) and protest (creating disruption through noise and physical presence where it is inconvenient for the boss). All these actions can be combined with fantastic communications on social media, in local newspapers and hopefully in the national press. If you take action, you should let the world know what you are doing. This can damage the reputation of your boss – which is often something they have a financial interest in maintaining! To complement action, you can always look into legal routes to turn that screw tighter as well. Legal action is certainly no replacement for action on the ground, but we can turn up the pressure by fighting an employer on all fronts. Again, research plays an important part in organizing, communications and legal strategies. This means getting your co-workers together and starting to look into the company, noting any weak points they may have, big events coming up or how much they make every year. Much of this will be public information.

Action is important because it is how we can win. Beyond this, though, action is crucial because it is transformative. Taking action changes workers – it is a learning process that builds networks, skills and confidence. However, in almost every mainstream union press release announcing strike action, we often see explanations like: 'we've been forced to strike', or that striking is the 'last resort'. Every time we see this, we cringe. Action builds organization. That using our power should be presented with regret, even by unions that benefit from that renewed organization, is outrageous. This thinking is, of course, a natural extension of the kind of union work in which paid officials negotiate on our behalf and attempt to settle a dispute with words as 'grown-ups', before either accepting a rubbish deal or putting workers into play as their pawns.

Rosa Luxemburg, a revolutionary socialist thinker, tells us that capitalism thrives when the ideas of the ruling class dominate our collective thinking. Such ruling-class ideas include the notion that anyone can do well under capitalism if they just work hard enough, or the thought that if we only could ask nicely for change then it might be granted. While we outnumber our bosses many, many times over, these ideas prevent us from putting in place a system that works for us. Luxemburg also shows us that mass action is the way to break this thinking. We have felt it in small ways ourselves, which is partly what motivated us to write this book. Every single person we interviewed for this book had felt this. Kickstarter workers expressed this feeling by saying 'we are forever changed', while Alex described it as taking the red pill in *The Matrix*. A taste of collective power is the antidote to feeling powerless under capitalism, more so than any explanation of how the system works.

This is why we talk about action as a learning process. Taking action yourself or supporting other workers' picket lines means being part of a 'living political school'.[2] Luxemburg explains that we can read many pamphlets or books (including, of course, one like this), but participating in this 'living political school' is critical for achieving change. In the workplace, this means that taking action can be a practical lesson. For example, 'the short strike is not only to pester the employer; it is like an army drill, to become the school of practice in preparation for the coming general or universal strike'.[3] In this context we can see that action should never be a last resort or a regret, but a key way in which we collectively develop our power. As Mildred, a cleaner from the LSE campaign, explained: 'I want everybody to be somebody like me, a hard fighter, a union fighter.'[4] That requires training, and the best training is going through a collective struggle.

12

THE RANK AND FILE

Although it is often the most important part of winning, organizing is not all about taking action. There are many things that have to happen in the run-up to successful action, as well as staying organized in between action and victories. As organizations grow and develop – from the workplace level to the larger trade unions – people begin to take on more specialised roles and positions. This happens whether those positions are formal or not. The temptation is to view this process of bureaucracy as something to be avoided at all costs. This is not surprising, given how many instances there are of bureaucrats selling out or undermining struggles. Anyone who has spent any time in a trade union will have come across people with this kind of bureaucratic mindset.

As discussed in chapter 10, the trade union bureaucracy serves a dual social function, and people often become part of the union bureaucracy for good reasons. Through their role, though, they come under pressure from employers and the state, so they can also be part of the way that workers in the movement are controlled. It is important to remember that creating relatively stable institutions of working-class power is an important step for the workers' movement. Trade unions are potential vehicles of struggle – both at high points and when the movement is at a low ebb. They have resources that can be put into struggles, connecting workplace campaigns across sectors, countries and even internationally. However, they can also act to undermine independent workers' action.

An argument we often hear is one that blames the bureaucracy for holding back struggles or preventing strikes from happening. In one sense, this is a reasonable critique to make. On the other hand, it is not in the interests of bureaucrats to put their careers and interests in the union at stake for a struggle they do not believe in. As Hal Draper reminds us, trade union bureaucracies differ from state or other institutional bureaucracies in one important way.[1] Trade union bureaucracies are caught between two competing pressures: that 'from above' – by employers, the state, the ruling class and others outside the working class and the membership of trade unions – and that 'from below', by workers and their membership. The struggle between these two antagonistic pressures shapes the bureaucracy. Unlike other institutions, if the trade union bureaucracy ignores the pressures from below entirely, there is a risk that workers will leave and stop paying their fees. This means that no matter how bureaucratic they may be, there is still a need to pay attention to workers' pressure from below – particularly during elections for union positions.

This means that a strategy that sees any bureaucratic development as something to be opposed misses an important dynamic of the workers' movement. While it would be great to have organizing that only involved large militant strikes and no need for structures to hold things together, in reality bureaucracy serves a function in maintaining trade unions. Instead, we need to critically understand what a trade union bureaucracy is. A point that we have returned to throughout the book remains key here: we have to understand the material interests of people involved. If we start from a materialist understanding of the trade union bureaucracy, we can find appropriate tactics and strategies to deal with bureaucrats when they come under pressure 'from above', searching for ways to apply our own pressure 'from below'.

In the longer term, this means rebuilding a confident rank and file that is capable of pressuring the bureaucracy to act in their interests. One perspective for doing this was put forward in a leaflet from the Clyde Workers' Committee in 1915:

We will support the officials just so long as they rightly represent the workers, but we will act independently immediately if they misrepresent them. Being composed of Delegates from every shop, and untrammelled by obsolete rule or law, we claim to represent the true feeling of the workers. We can act immediately according to the merits of the case and the desire of the rank and file.[2]

This is the principle of organizing as rank-and-file workers: cooperating with the bureaucracy when it aids struggle, but acting independently when needed.

We tried to apply these principles during the University and College Union campaign over the USS university pension scheme in 2018. The UCU was the product of a merger in 2006. The former general secretary of one of the unions, Sally Hunt, became leader of the UCU, making her a leader who was not only removed from the experiences of the workplace but who had never experienced them in the first place. As she explained: 'I don't pretend to be an academic. I never have been . . . I wouldn't expect them to have to go and do a negotiation. Equally, I think they don't need me to be running seminars.'[3] This is a clear example of the professionalization of the bureaucracy in the UCU.

There had been a long dispute over the pension scheme, with strikes in 2010–11 that ended in a major concession to employers. The union accepted a deal for a two-tiered pension scheme, with worse conditions for new joiners. Further strikes failed to prevent more concessions to employers, and workers saw their pay decline throughout the period. There was increasing anger from the membership, particularly after the union called two-hour lunchtime strikes in 2014. Overall, these micro-strikes simply led to the docking of pay without having any impact on the running of the university.

By 2018, the stage was set for a longer confrontation with employers. Across 61 universities there was a plan for an

escalating series of strike days to take place over four weeks
– far more action than had been called previously. In preparation for the strikes, we started a workplace bulletin called
'The University Worker' through *Notes from Below*.[4] The
plan was to address the lack of communication from the
national union, sharing experiences, tactics and strategies
between members.

The bulletin provided a way to reach out to active members
across the different campuses and collect reports from them.
For some issues of the bulletin, we received way too many
reports for a two-pager and had to add extra reports and
pictures online. It was one small step towards forming
networks that were separate from the union bureaucracy.
The PDF format allowed hundreds to be printed off around
the UK, while we handed them out at five London universities. The bulletin also became a focus for discussions about
how the dispute was going, hosting arguments about what
the next steps could be.

During the dispute, it began to look like victory might be
possible, as some employers started to break. Despite this, a
potential deal was proposed between the union and
Universities UK (the organization of the employers). We
published a special issue of the bulletin a day later, calling the
deal a 'sell out'. A rumour spread that the union leadership
could only be proposing a deal so bad as to send some sort of
secret message to the membership – imagine! As we wrote
about at the time, the conspiracy theory was popular with the
more conservative parts of the membership, who could not

seem to believe the union bureaucracy would consider a deal like this.[5] Given the failure of campaigns over the past decade, it should have come as no surprise that a union bureaucracy so far removed from the experiences of either the university or the picket lines had such a low horizon.

In response, we started a petition to reject the deal. It was signed by more than 10,000 members, and fifty branches voted for the rejection. We called a demonstration outside the UCU headquarters. When we arrived at the headquarters in London there was palpable frustration across the gathered crowd. Most of the members present were younger or earlier in their careers, so they were much more likely to be in the lower tier of the pension scheme – many not even opting to pay in as their wages were so low. We saw the front door of the union office was ajar. Channelling our student experiences of occupying universities many years before, we rushed into the foyer of the building. Outraged union staff told us to leave immediately, threatening to call the police. The flash occupation was one example of that pressure 'from below' that members can exert on the bureaucracy. The crowd gathered around the office, with members tapping pound coins on the windows to indicate who the union should belong to. While bureaucrats and officials discussed the future of the pension scheme upstairs, the demonstration – which was literally 'below' – fought against the deal.

The dispute did not end with the sell-out deal; the negotiators hastily rejected it because of the push back. Instead, it ended in a draw: the union accepted a proposal for a so-called 'joint expert panel' that would investigate the pension scheme. The panel was formed half from the union and half from the employers, with an 'independent chair'. We opposed this deal too, but it was accepted by the membership. As we write, the dispute is continuing with another round of strikes. The joint expert panel went nowhere, and the chair voted with the employers every single time.

We have chosen this example not because it is a perfect example of rank-and-file organizing, but because it illustrates the complications and contradictions of trying to implement a strategy like this. Despite our reservations about the tactics and strategy for the dispute, a national campaign opened up the space for new kinds of rank-and-file action. Having picket lines at universities across the country provided the opportunity to distribute the bulletin as well as a focus for the debates. More importantly, it moved many members into action. This meant organizing meetings, calling members, getting the vote out for the strike and organizing picket lines. Action, as we discussed earlier in the chapter, builds confidence, consciousness and combativity. The national strike raised the potential of a new rank and file in the union, something that had not existed for a long time.

'The University Worker' was not the only attempt to do something different during the dispute – neither are we arguing that it was decisive in shaping the outcome. What we are trying to say is that we should find ways to engage with the bureaucracy while also trying to build power independent of it. We started writing the bulletin as a way to engage rank-and-file members in what was happening, as well as encouraging activists to debate tactics and strategy. It brought together a small layer of organizers who may not otherwise have been in contact.

The emergence of a new layer of activists during the dispute meant that trying to organize independently of the bureaucracy was now a possibility. The tensions with bureaucrats – whether over the failure to communicate effectively, put forward a strategy for the dispute or consider deals from the employers – provided something against which to organize. This new rank-and-file militancy was born in the petitions, demonstrations and pressure from below. It may not have resulted in an overwhelming victory of the membership in the dispute, but it shifted the campaign. When Sally Hunt stepped down as general secretary, the independent Jo Grady was able to win, beating both the established left and right candidates in the election. The suspension of strike action meant that the rank and file fell away, not being sustained in any of the new or existing formations inside the union machinery. However, it meant that when new strikes were called, the experiences and learnings of the previous dispute were put back into action.

The example shows the necessity of trying to organize as rank and file during a dispute, as well as the many challenges this can involve. In a national campaign like this, there are really two interrelated fights. The first is the fight with the employers. A strike is a clash of opposing interests, settled when one side gives up. For the employer this can mean that the costs of the strike outweigh the concessions. Strikes are, of course, about material interests. This is also the case with the second fight: between the rank and file and the bureaucracy of the union. During a strike the bureaucracy comes under increasing pressure from the employers – as well as potentially from other outside forces like the state. Even if there is a 'good' bureaucrat, they will start to face increasing pressure. As the bureaucracy mediates between the employer and workers, they ultimately have an interest in settling the dispute. Their economic interest is in a settlement that is acceptable to both members and employers. If the pressure from employers outweighs that from the membership, they can propose 'sell-out' deals like that discussed earlier. The fight between the interests of the rank and file and the employers with the bureaucracy therefore shapes how the campaign will be carried out by the union. Winning this second fight is about getting the kind of action and support from the union that can effectively win the first fight with employers.

It is important to remember that we are not trying to build perfect trade unions. Instead, we want to build unions as vehicles of struggle that can fight in the here and now, as well as help us along the way to fighting for much more. It means searching for ways to build power from below that can exert pressure on the bureaucracy, as well as acting independently when we need to. It means taking on the bureaucracy politically, not falling into blaming them for acting in their own interests. It also means that when we are organizing, we need to constantly ask ourselves how any actions we are taking build confidence in the rank and file.

13
DEMOCRACY

Democracy is, of course, closely related to the issues of bureaucracy and the rank and file, and it is a key way we can exert pressure 'from below' on the bureaucracy. However, there is a risk that we start to think of democracy in the abstract. We need to fight for democratic trade unions, but this will not stop bureaucracy, only help to keep it in check.

Although democracy is an ideal in and of itself that should exist throughout our organizing, we want to focus on democracy as a tool of organizing for two important reasons. First, democracy is a practical necessity to win. Focusing on union structure risks missing a crucial aspect of democracy in organizing. Democracy matters because it is how we win campaigns. If we launch a campaign on our own without speaking to anyone about it, we would have to win it on our own. By building a campaign democratically that has mass support, including an active and united workforce that has decided on the demand and believes in it, we are far more likely to win. At the very heart of this has to be a democratic decision. What shall we demand? What are we going to do to win it? This democratic decision needs to be a real, active and genuine one, not simply a proposal by one person who then tallies up symbolic 'yes' votes.

This is where democracy serves a crucial function in organizing and winning. If we want to develop our collective power, however, it is not just about winning but also about developing worker organizers along the way. This brings us to the second reason democracy is an important tool of organizing. Across society, we have very little formal say in most decisions that affect us. The chance to put a cross in a box every five years is a poor substitute. If we as workers do not have a say in campaigns about our conditions, there is little opportunity for us to have a say in anything else. Organizing is about developing our confidence as workers to have a say over how we work, something that needs to be fought for through action.

Democracy is essential for winning, but also for building socialism. Without democracy in our unions or organizations we are not building the tools that we need to win at work, let alone overthrow capitalism. Democracy in this sense is how we build leaders and how we build our own networks of working-class power.

We also want to emphasise that democracy is a messy and complicated process in practice. We deal with the unevenness of experience, the ideas of the ruling class, the lack of worker confidence and many other issues in the process. But democracy is also an opportunity. We should not be scared to put forward our ideas, even if they are rejected.

Our campaigns need to position democracy at the forefront. To fight for democratic workplaces we need to have not just union staffers or a single elected official but collective leadership of workers. As Hal Draper argues:

> socialism can be realized only through the self-emancipation of activized masses in motion, reaching out for freedom with their own hands, mobilized 'from below' in a struggle to take charge of their own destiny, as actors (not merely subjects) on the stage of history.[1]

He contrasts this with a long history of emancipation 'from above', whether through appeals to lords, messiahs or other 'good' rulers. Draper's point is that emancipation is only possible through the self-activity of those striving to be emancipated. This is not some sort of purist position, but that it is in the process of struggle that liberation happens.

The fight against one boss is therefore a part of the overall struggle for emancipation. The skill, experience and confidence that is built in a single fight feeds into the future battles, whether there is victory in the moment or not. The risk is that we lose sight of the process of struggle and focus only on the outcomes. Of course, winning a pay rise or better conditions is important. What is more important, though, is that through the process of fighting, workers experience self-change. Struggle is a learning process. It forges new leaders, organization and raises the horizons of what can be fought over.

If we focus only on the outcomes, we risk missing the importance of this process. One risk is that we give leadership to the bureaucracy, a seasoned activist or some politically savvy operator. Instead of building collective power, we develop a leadership which acts on the behalf of the membership. While this may win something at work, it does not build the capacity for us to win more than that. It hands down victories to the membership without building their capacity to fight for more.

As Marx once noted, being determines consciousness. It is through our experiences and struggles that ideas change, not the other way round. The problem is that these experiences are rarely even. This unevenness means that some leaders are developed more than others, or experiences are not shared more widely. Taking on positions – whether official or through our own place in a struggle – means that unevenness can develop further, restricting access to knowledge, power and resources for the wider membership. In positions of power, people can focus on just getting things done, rather than thinking about how they are done. We can certainly say the two of us have been guilty of this.

While we obviously care deeply about winning improvements in terms and conditions, it is the journey of getting there that will prepare us collectively to overcome capitalism. A campaign run behind the scenes by a couple of dedicated activists, but with limited participation by the whole group of workers, may win. But at the end of the day the group of workers has not become confident in running a campaign.

They did not have to write their own press releases, or organize a ballot, they just had to show up.

For those with more experience or more time, when we find ourselves doing things for others that they could have done themselves, we must bring ourselves back to the principle that our liberatory project is based on mass action and self-emancipation. Organizing without these building blocks makes it harder to defend our victories or build towards systemic change. This does not mean that as organizers in our workplaces we have to be wallflowers, hoping for an 'authentic' workplace leader to spontaneously come into being. In fact, showing courage and leadership helps build other leaders. It does mean, though, that education should always be a core part of our organizing. At a well-organized workplace, if a key organizer should leave, they should have already passed on their knowledge and skills to many others.

It is not through debate alone that we are going to build another world. Through the practice of workplace struggle we are forming the seeds of what an alternative society could look like. Organizing is an experiment with this. When we debate with other workers, build our own structures and take action together, we are building our capacity for struggle. In the heat of a strike, we need to make sure we are collectively able to withstand the loss of our wages. These moments of collective solidarity give us a glimpse of what that alternative could look like.

14

THE BIGGER HORIZON

We can catch sight of radical democracy 137 years before the sans-papier movement broke out on the streets of Paris. In 1871, the Paris Commune, a worker-led insurrection 'transformed the city of Paris into an autonomous Commune and set about improvising the free organization of its social life according to principles of association and cooperation'.[1]

There had been a wave of democratic revolutions across Europe, including in France in 1848. The working-class movement had been defeated and a military dictatorship established. In the run-up to the commune, working-class radicalization returned. In 1870, the Franco-Prussian war broke out. As the Prussian army approached Paris, the government enlisted workers into the ranks of the National Guard. Paris was quickly besieged from all sides. Once it became clear the French government could not defend Paris, a surrender was agreed and the Prussian army ended the siege. Within the city, a dispute broke out between the French government and workers in the National Guard over who should control cannons left over at the end of the war. The government's army intervened, attempting to seize the cannons from workers. This led to a confrontation in which two French generals were captured and executed. The army quickly withdrew to Versailles. Workers and the National Guard took over Paris, erecting barricades and taking control of key buildings. The central committee of the National Guard met in Hôtel de Ville, with a red flag raised over the building, to prepare for elections.

On 26 March 1871, elections were held for ninety-two members of the Commune council, one for every 20,000 residents in Paris. This established a workers' republic: the Paris Commune. They voted to waive rents during the siege, took over abandoned workplaces and ran them as co-ops, redistributed unoccupied housing, stopped fines and the docking of wages, banned night shifts for bakers, fixed the price of bread, made education free, set civil servant wages at the average workers' rate, dissolved the army and armed the people. This was the first time that many of these demands had been raised by a popular movement, and they were ground-breaking, demonstrating what a democratically organized community could look like. It allowed the workers, now known as the Communards, to shape the conditions of their own lives.

While the Communards were experimenting with what an alternative society could look like in Paris, the French army was preparing. Having retreated to Versailles, they began preparing for a counter-offensive. By 2 April, the army started bombing Paris and the city was under siege again.

The army entered the city on 21 May. They spent eight days massacring workers. An estimated 30,000 Communards were executed, with many others deported or imprisoned.

There are at least two important lessons we can take from the Paris Commune. The first is that it provides a practical instance of how working-class struggle can attempt to overthrow capitalist social relations through revolution. As Marx remarked, 'working men's Paris, with its Commune, will be forever celebrated as the glorious harbinger of a new society. Its martyrs are enshrined in the great heart of the working class.'[2] It provides a powerful example of what is possible, but also a warning of how it can end. The Paris Commune lasted only 72 days. As reported in *Der Sozialdemokrat*: there was 'a sea of blood separating two worlds; on the one side, those who struggled for a different and better world, and on the other, those who sought to preserve the old order'.[3]

The spirit of the commune appears again and again in the years that followed, both in raising similar demands for the radical democratization of society as well as in the ferocity with which the ruling class fought back. Marx, in a revised preface to the *Communist Manifesto* published in 1872, argued that 'one thing especially was proved by the Commune' – that 'the working class cannot simply lay hold of the ready-made state machinery, and wield it for its own purposes'.[4] The Commune shows how overthrowing capitalism requires the creation of a new way of organizing society, not merely seizing the structures of the ruling class. It also requires defending it.

We can see small moments of the Commune again throughout the history that follows. There are also times where it breaks through in mass struggle, although none of these have led to lasting changes. It can be seen clearly again in 1905 in Russia: the start of a revolutionary process, with huge strikes breaking out across the country and mutinies in the military. Workers began forming soviets – workers' councils – often at the factory level. These were democratic bodies that operated autonomously, organizing strikes and direct action. Despite this wave of struggle, the Tsar was able to avert revolution through desperate reforms. However, by 1917 the Tsar had abdicated and soviets had sprung up again across Russia. The soviets became an alternative power to the provisional government that had been established. The Bolsheviks proposed the overthrowing of the provisional government by transferring 'all power to the soviets'.

The revolution led to a series of widespread changes in Russia. First, Russia withdrew from World War One. The army was restructured, abolishing all ranks of corporal and above. Banks and other key industries were taken under democratic control. Land was transferred to peasants and workers took control of the means of production and distribution. Widespread social insurance was introduced. Decrees outlawing inequality based on gender, nationality and religion were issued, among many other changes. These changes radically reshaped Russia. However, almost immediately the revolution came under attack. An Allied intervention was led by Britain and France, and the civil war that followed strangled the revolution. While the Soviet Republic continued, the base of the revolution was destroyed. Stalin was able to come to power, crushing his opposition and establishing a form of 'state capitalism'.[5] In the brief time workers were in power, though, they showed that another world was possible.

Starting in the 1930s, there was a wave of struggle across Spain, including mass strikes and land seizures. Two major unions played an important role: the CNT (Confederación Nacional del Trabajo), an anarchist confederation of local industrial unions, and the UGT (Unión General de Trabajadores) aligned with the PSOE (Partido Socialista Obrero Español) that also had Communist Party members involved. Following the election of left-wing Republicans in 1936, the army launched a coup. Nationalists fought against Republicans for control of the country, and Spain was plunged into civil war. In around two-thirds of Spain the coup was initially pushed back. In Barcelona, the CNT led the resistance, setting off sirens in factories and organizing hundreds of neighbourhood defence groups. Factories were seized and used to arm the anti-fascist militias. In areas held by the Republicans a social revolution began, with democratic assemblies established in workplaces, neighbourhoods and villages. Unions established their own armies to fight the military. Despite the workers' struggles, disputes between sections of the left – particularly the Stalinist-aligned Communist Party – led to the undermining of the revolution. The civil war would end with Franco taking control of the country and establishing a fascist dictatorship.[6] There was another glimpse of workers' power that ended too soon.

In the 1960s, there was a wave of revolutionary and anti-colonial struggles. The spirit of the Commune came back to France, and starting in May 1968, students occupied universities and organized demonstrations. Faced with a wave of police repression, trade unions called for sympathy strikes in solidarity with students. The strikes spread quickly, with around 9 million workers involved. Workers occupied factories, and neither the trade unions nor political parties could control the militancy from below. At the end of May, the president, Charles de Gaulle, fled France, fearing the protest would turn to revolution. While there was a moment where the Commune could have been repeated, neither the Communist Party nor other revolutionary parties escalated. An election was called, order restored and the revolutionary moment faded away.[7]

In Italy, the 'Hot Autumn' of 1968 saw a wave of wildcat strikes and protests, leading to a period of militant worker organizing. There followed similar moments of 'revolutionary rehearsals', including Chile in 1972–1973, Portugal 1974–1975, Iran 1979 and Poland 1980–1981.[8] From the 1980s onwards, many have tried to argue that workers no longer have the power, interest or inclination for struggles like these – or that workers no longer exist. However, at the end of 2010, protests brought down the government in Tunisia. In 2011, a wave of struggles broke across the Middle East and North Africa. In Egypt, the street protests and occupation of

Tahrir Square spread into strikes, forcing Mubarak's resignation. Across the region, protestors and workers fought corrupt regimes. In some countries this involved a resurgence of the labour movement, now able to organize publicly.

As the Arab Spring spread to Syria in 2011, the Assad dictatorship began a brutal crackdown on protests. As fighting intensified in Aleppo, Syrian troops were pulled out of the north of Syria. The Kurdish Democratic Union Party (PYD) announced regional autonomy across Rojava in 2014. Elections were held and a new constitution approved. The Constitution of Rojava guarantees cultural, religious and political freedoms while explicitly aiming to end gender discrimination. The model of governance that has emerged emphasises grassroots democracy and participation, inspired by the libertarian socialist turn of imprisoned Kurdish leader Abdullah Öcalan. This has seen the establishment of worker cooperatives, direct democracy through district and civil councils, and restorative justice. The experiment with a new way of running society within Rojava has not happened in isolation. From 2013 onwards, the YPG (People's Defense Units) has fought Islamist factions, including the Islamic State of Iraq and the Levant (ISIL) which launched a siege of Kobanî in 2014. On the other side, Rojava is bordered by Turkey, which has a long history of oppressing the Kurds. Turkey considers both the PYD and YPG to be the same as the Kurdistan Workers' Party (PKK), which it lists as a terrorist organization. It should therefore come as no surprise that Turkey opposed their actions in Rojava and attacked

YPG forces, using artillery and air strikes. Within this context, the social revolution taking place in Rojava is hemmed in with violence from all sides. Despite this, it again demonstrates what radical change can look like in practice.[9]

Each of these examples shows us moments of workers trying to take control over their lives. The spirit of the Commune can be seen each time, whether in the demands or in the brutal repression that follows. It should not come as much surprise to hear that none of these were straightforward attempts. As Lenin argued, 'whoever expects a "pure" social revolution will *never* live to see it. Such a person pays lip-service to revolution without understanding what revolution is.'[10] Instead, revolutions come with the contradictions and chaos of people trying to free themselves from capitalism. They each form part of a much longer global history of the oppressed and exploited rising up. From slave revolts to farmer protests, strikes, occupations and rebellions, there is a still unfinished history of struggle from below.[11] We often are not taught this history growing up – or if we are, we are taught a version that is stripped of its radical content. It is also important to remember that there is a rich history of struggles below the surface that are never reported.

Organizing at work may seem incredibly distant to these revolutionary struggles. However, the high points of revolutionary struggle are generally accompanied by high levels of organization from below. Whether these involve soviets, workers' councils, assemblies or other forms of direct democracy, they form the basic element of building working-class power. The lack of effective organizing at the base has held the workers' movement back at critical moments, whether in elections, pushing back against governments or in revolutionary moments. We should therefore know that organizing in your own job, no matter how difficult or disconnected it may seem, is part of building towards a more democratic future. After all, as David Graeber once argued:

> The ultimate, hidden truth of the world is that it is something that we make, and could just as easily make differently . . . It only exists because every day we wake up and continue to produce it. If we woke up one morning and all collectively decided to produce something else, then we wouldn't have capitalism anymore.[12]

The key question is, then: how we get to that moment of collective decision?

Not everyone who is organizing at work has sight of a bigger horizon, whether fighting for a different kind of world or not. In many cases people are organizing to push back against the worst parts of their jobs or defend benefits that they may have. The leap to organizing for a better world can often seem very far away from where we are today. However, the shoots of the socialist future break through the surface in our workplace struggles. The key is how we encourage them to grow.

Conclusion:
PUTTING TROUBLEMAKING INTO PRACTICE

Throughout this book we have argued for troublemaking and organizing at work. There is, nonetheless, no simple recipe or solution for how you can start doing that. Each workplace is unique and will have its particular challenges. However, we can be certain of three points that can help you to organize. First, if you want to win at work, you will need to take action. Strikes should not be thought of as a last-ditch option. Action brings workers together and it demonstrates our power. It is a learning process. Depending on the context of your organizing, you will likely encounter some kind of bureaucracy. We cannot avoid bureaucracy, but instead we need to find ways to build pressure 'from below' and develop rank-and-file confidence. This means thinking about the material interests of bureaucrats and the employers and taking seriously how our actions build power against both. Finally, we need to make democracy a core part of our organizing. Not as an abstract principle, but from understanding the central importance of worker self-activity in organizing and winning. Yes, we want to win, but we also want to develop the confidence of workers to fight to democratise workplaces and society more widely.

There are many excellent resources on the 'how to' of organizing – see some examples in the 'get organized' section and the list of further reading after this chapter. We consider the previous sections to be principles that guide our own troublemaking. Often this means taking inspiration or learning from the different 'how-to' guides and reapplying it. For workplace organizing, this means taking into account at least three different factors. First, 'the nature of the times' and whether there is a low or high level of class struggle. The wider context in which organizing is taking place matters, shaping the tactics and strategies that can be used. The second is 'the nature of the industry'. What works in one kind of job or sector of the economy might not work elsewhere. We need to think seriously about the dynamics of the work and what kinds of tactics can be used with the technical composition of our work. The third factor is the 'tradition and structure of the union' we organize in. It may be that it is a large and bureaucratic union with huge resources or a smaller and (potentially) more democratic organization. This will affect the orientation we take towards the union structures. The fourth is whether 'there's already a movement to which you have to relate, or whether it's a question of initiating such a movement'.[1] Hal Draper explains that each of these factors will shape the issues you face when organizing in practice. There is, unfortunately, no *one* way to do it successfully.

Given that there is no organizing recipe book, we must instead find a method that can guide us across different contexts. Throughout this book we have provided the concepts to critically make sense of different kinds of work, examples of struggles in various sectors of work, and principles to guide organizing. Taken together, these form the outline of a potential method. The key is testing this in practice, through talking to co-workers, investigating your conditions of work and then trying to do something about them. The 'doing something about them' is troublemaking that focuses on taking action, building rank-and-file power and making sure the process is democratic.

We can have the power to collectively shape our lives and the future. As C.L.R. James put it: 'every cook can govern'.[2] The key to getting there is workers' self-activity. While some have written off workers' ability to change the world, as Martin Glaberman reminds us, 'one thing that I think is an absolute given: workers will resist, because work sucks. Until someone can tell me that work has become real nice under capitalism, whether in the United States or anywhere else, I say that is the fundamental basis of our theory and our practice. Work sucks and sooner or later workers are going to resist it in whatever way they can.'[3] There are three important constants of work. First, work is necessarily antagonistic. When looked at in general, it is a process through which one class exploits another. In the case of a specific workplace, it means that work is alive with the struggle between the competing interests. Second, work brings workers into contact with others with shared interests. We meet other people and have something in common. This provides a point from which collective struggles can develop. Third, workers' struggles offer glimpses of another kind of world. Our struggles at work are collective. When we fight for control of our own workplaces, we are engaging in democratic struggle. When we strike, we need to cooperate. These struggles provide a collective learning experience that points towards a different way of organizing society.

An increasing number of people agree with the idea that capitalism cannot continue. It is destroying our lives, communities, the environment and the future. If we want revolutionary change, the process through which we get there is important. We will not have an alternative system handed down to us, neither can it simply be voted for. As Marx argued, 'the emancipation of the working class must be the act of the working class itself.'[4] In practice, this means we need to find ways to connect the small fights in an individual workplace up to the bigger questions of social change.

We are often told that economic and political struggles are separate. This view holds that strike action can be used to negotiate a better deal at work, yet we should not use that power to change society. We are told to leave political questions to parties and voting, and in many contexts, the law is used to ban political strikes – unions deal with economic questions and parliament deals with political questions. This hamstrings us from dealing effectively with either. Instead, we need to find a way to overcome this separation between economics and politics.

You should organize at work, but we cannot leave politics to politicians. Instead, we need to find new ways to connect economic and political struggles. As Rosa Luxemburg argued: 'the economic struggle is the transmitter from one political centre to another; the political struggle is the periodic fertilization of the soil for the economic struggle. Cause and effect here continually change places.'[5] She saw the high point of this in mass strikes. To understand what this means today, we need to understand how class composition has changed. We have both been inspired by Marx's simple workers' inquiry questionnaire from 1880. In the short text that accompanies it, Marx lays out the challenges that faced socialists then, which are still so pressing today. If we want to overcome capitalism, we need to identify the power that can transform society. Workers build and rebuild society every day, from creating and maintaining the infrastructure, goods and services, to undertaking the domestic work and care we all rely upon. We already understand how to run society. We make the things and provide the services, we need; we could do this for ourselves. Understanding our conditions and struggles should be the central question facing socialists. It is through this process that we can find the answers to our questions.

Of course, the survey is not the only tool to do this. Today we have many more ways we can explore these issues at work together. This means thinking about your own work, the work of people you know or going out and talking to other people. Class composition provides a powerful way to understand our struggles at work, starting with the technical composition, or the actual conditions there, then moving to social composition, drawing out from the workplace to our wider communities and society. This means taking into account the way we live outside of work, with our relationship to housing, services, the state and oppression. Taken together, both of these provide the basis from which new forms of political composition can emerge. This is not as an automatic relationship, but a leap to new ways of resisting and organizing. A first step means taking seriously how different moments of class composition matter. It is on this basis that we can develop tactics and strategies that actually work.

We all want the excitement of seeing socialist ideas put into practice. The election campaigns of Bernie Sanders and Jeremy Corbyn provided clear examples of how an alternative can inspire hundreds of thousands of new socialists. Yet the failure of both these electoral projects risks a turn towards defeatism. As Sai Englert has argued, the situation today is

> highly contradictory: both full of opportunity and repeated major political set-backs. This state of affairs is especially dangerous for a political tradition that bases its liberatory project on the mass action, and ultimate self-emancipation, of the working class. It leads activists all around us to pessimisms, demobilisation, and/or – much worse – a moralistic sense of

superiority that dismisses the very people on which the success of our struggles depends, as inherently reactionary, backwards, or unorganisable.[6]

The antidote to this is troublemaking at work. The left needs to move away from speaking only to the rest of the left, casting blame on each other. Instead, we need more workplace militants and organizers.

When we talk about struggle as a process of transformation, this applies to everyone involved. It is not about 'going door-to-door and making workers into ideal socialists. You've got to take workers as they are, with all their contradictions, with all their nonsense. But the fact that society forces them to struggle begins to transform the working class.'[7] None of us are born perfect revolutionaries. Instead, we deal with the concrete situation that faces us. The way we struggle to transform it begins to change us too. We may well come across reactionary ideas when we are organizing. By challenging these in practice, we can begin to form the kind of politics that can fight oppression and build solidarity. Through each strike and campaign, we can learn something new as individuals as well as being part of collective transformation.

This means starting where we already are. Even if your own workplace does not seem like the best place to start organizing, have a go at it. Help others to start organizing. We still think that 'As We See It' from *Solidarity* is a great starting point. 'Meaningful action', they argue, 'is whatever increases the confidence, the autonomy, the initiative, the participation, the solidarity, the equalitarian tendencies and the self-activity of the masses and whatever assists in their demystification.' This is what we should be aiming to do, whether big or small. We should also avoid 'sterile and harmful action', that is, 'whatever reinforces the passivity of the masses, their apathy, their cynicism, their differentiation through hierarchy, their alienation, their reliance on others to do things for them and the degree to which they can therefore be manipulated by others – even by those allegedly acting on their behalf'.[8]

This means getting involved with troublemaking while keeping those broader horizons in sight. This might be starting something new or joining something ongoing. The one thing we can guarantee is that it will not be straightforward. We, as workers, have insights into our work and the potential power to change it. That does not mean we will get on with each other or that we will not have to deal with contradictions and difficult situations. We may join a radical union or one that has suffered from bureaucratization. In the struggle for another kind of world we cannot wait for the perfect weapons, for everyone to get trained or build the perfect union structure – we need to use what is available to us. Troublemaking is always messy. We can take the principles for organizing as an aim, but not let them hold us back. The most important thing is testing our ideas in practice.

There is no point debating the ideal tactics or strategies disconnected from action. Organizing at work can be a practical school of class struggle, but we have to be there to learn. If we want an alternative to capitalism it will start from day-to-day struggles in the workplace. We cannot achieve long-lasting change without striking at the heart of capitalism. Every victory, from pushing back against one manager to raising conditions across a sector, is a step forward. This alone will not change society. As Lenin reminds us, a revolutionary situation involves a crisis from above and below: 'it is usually insufficient for "the lower classes not to want" to live in the old way; it is also necessary that "the upper classes should be unable" to live in the old way.'⁹ We cannot get to this moment through troublemaking at work alone. History tells us that these moments happen again and again – so, when the next one comes, we need to be as organized as possible. It is then we can not only try to change the course of capitalism, but consign it to history. This begins with you talking to your co-workers.

GET ORGANIZED

If you want to start getting organized at work, you can sign up for support with two projects.

In the UK, you can sign up to Organize Now! It is a project organized by the Bakers, Food and Allied Workers Union (BFAWU), Strike Map and Notes from Below. Built by workers for workers, it is a peer to peer organizing network responding to the crises in work, pay and living standards. Skilled and experienced organizers from across sectors are available to help you and your co-workers organize to defend and improve your working lives and build power. They arrange coaching calls by phone to talk through the steps to organize at work.

- Sign up at organizenow.org.uk

In the US, you can sign up to the Emergency Workplace Organizing Committee (EWOC). It is a project organized by the Democratic Socialists of America (DSA) and the United Electrical, Radio and Machine Workers of America (UE). They are building a distributed, grassroots organizing programme to support workers organizing at the workplace. They will connect you with a workplace organizer to learn more about how you and your co-workers can improve your working conditions.

- Sign up at workerorganizing.org

If you have experience organizing at work already, you can sign up to volunteer with Organize Now! or EWOC. If you are interested in starting something similar in another country, get in touch.

FURTHER READING

Aaron Brenner, Robert Brenner and Cal Winslow, *Rebel Rank and File: Labor Militancy and Revolt from Below During the Long 1970s*. London: Verso, 2010.

Alexandra Bradbury, Mark Brenner and Jane Slaughter, *Secrets of a Successful Organizer* (Labor Notes, 2016), labornotes.org/secrets.

Amelia Horgan, *Lost in Work: Escaping Capitalism*. London: Pluto, 2021.

Aziz Choudry and Mondli Hlatshwayo, *Just Work?: Migrant Workers' Struggles Today*. London: Pluto, 2015.

Clark McAllister, *Karl Marx's Workers' Inquiry: International History, Reception, and Responses*. London: Notes from Below, 2022.

Dario Azzellini and Immanuel Ness, *Ours to Master and to Own: Workers' Control from the Commune to the Present*. Chicago: Haymarket, 2013.

Eric Blanc, *Red State Revolt: The Teachers' Strike Wave and Working-Class Politics*. London, Verso, 2019.

Eve Livingston, *Make Bosses Pay: Why We Need Unions*. London: Pluto, 2021.

Gavin Mueller, *Breaking Things At Work: The Luddites Were Right About Why You Hate Your Job*. London: Verso, 2021.

Ian Allinson, *Workers Can Win: A Guide to Organizing at Work*. London: Pluto, 2022.

Immanuel Ness, *Organizing Insurgency: Workers' Movements in the Global South*. London: Pluto, 2021.

Industrial Workers of the World (UK), 'Resources', IWW, 2022, iww.org.uk.

Jane Hardy, *Nothing to Lose But Our Chains: Work and Resistance in Twenty-First-Century Britain*. London: Pluto, 2021.

Jane Holgate, *Arise: Power, Strategy and Union Resurgence*. London: Pluto, 2021.

Jane McAlevey, *No Shortcuts: Organizing for Power in the New Gilded Age*. Oxford: Oxford University Press, 2016.

Joe Burns, *Class Struggle Unionism*. Chicago: Haymarket, 2022.

Karl Marx, *Capital: A Critique of Political Economy, Volume 1*, London: Penguin, 1990.

Kim Moody, *On New Terrain: How Capital is Reshaping the Battleground of Class War*. Chicago: Haymarket, 2017.

Notes from Below, *From the Workplace: A Collection of Worker Writing*. London: Notes from Below, 2020.

Notes from Below, 2022, notesfrombelow.org.

Organizing Work, 2022, https://organizing.work.

Ralph Darlington, *Radical Unionism: The Rise and Fall of Revolutionary Syndicalism*. Chicago: Haymarket, 2013.

Richard Hyman, *Strikes*. London: Palgrave Macmillan, 1989.

Worker Organizing, 'Resources', 2022, workplaceorganizing.uk.

NOTES

Introduction

1 Institute for Economic Affairs, '67 Per Cent of Young Brits Want a Socialist Economic System, Finds New Poll', 2021, iea.org.uk.
2 Laura Wronski, 'Axios/Momentive Poll: Capitalism and Socialism', Surveymonkey, 2021, surveymonkey.com.
3 UCL, 'What UCL Does', 2021, ucl.ac.uk.

1 No Excuses

1 Alex Marshall, 'Notes from the Road', *Notes from Below*, 7 October 2020, notesfrombelow.org.
2 Ibid.
3 Ibid.
4 A limb (b) worker is an intermediate employment status in the UK, between employee and self-employed, in which the worker is a 'dependent contractor' and gains access to some basic employment rights.
5 Marshall, 'Notes from the Road'.
6 KVSS, 'Kachra Vahatuk Shramik Sangh', 2021, kvssmumbai.weebly.com.
7 Quoted in Chandan Khanna, 'For India's Caste-Based Sewer Cleaners, an Uncertain Robot Rescue', *Undark*, 20 September 2019, undark.org.
8 Safai Karmachari Andolan, 'Crisis', 2021, safaikarmachariandolan.org.
9 Quoted in Khanna, 'For India's Caste-Based Sewer Cleaners'.
10 KVSS, 'Kachra Vahatuk Shramik Sangh'.

11 Sujatha Fernandes, 'How Mumbai's Sanitation Workers Won Their Rights', *The Nation*, 5 March 2019, thenation.com.

12 Ibid.

13 Quoted in ibid.

14 Quoted in ibid.

2 Fighting for Control

1 German Lopez, 'I was Skeptical of Unions. Then I Joined One', *Vox*, 19 August 2019, vox.com.

2 ONS, 'Ethnicity Pay Gaps: 2019', Office for National Statistics, 2019, ons.gov.uk.; ONS, 'Gender Pay Gap in the UK: 2021', Office for National Statistics, 2021, ons.gov.uk.

3 Aziz Hasan, 'A Message to Our Community', *Kickstarter*, 27 September 2019, kickstarter.com.

4 Quoted in Brian Menegus, 'Leaked Memo Shows Kickstart Senior Staffers Are Pushing Back Against Colleagues' Union Efforts', *Gizmodo*, 21 March 2019, gizmodo.com.

5 Kickstarter Union Oral History, 'Introducing the Kickstarter Oral History', Engelberg Center NYU School of Law, 22 September 2020, eclive.engelberg.center.

6 Kickstarter Union Oral History, 'The Pandemic', Engelberg Center NYU School of Law, 27 April 2021, eclive.engelberg.center.

3 Winning Big

1 Quoted in Lydia Hughes and Achille Marotta, 'Rebellion at the LSE: A Cleaning Sector Inquiry', *Notes from Below*, 9 February 2018, notesfrombelow.org.

2 *The Guardian*, 'Fight for Your Rights: The Trade Union for Outsourced Workers', *YouTube*, 12 August 2020, youtube.com/ watch?v=asUEj0uCpjE.

3 *The Guardian*, 'Fight for Your Rights'.

4 Ibid.

5 United Voices of the World, 'Sodexo and St Mary's Hospital Shame on You!', *Facebook*, 23 October 2019, facebook.com.

6 We would recommend watching the *Guardian*'s 'Fight for Your Rights' documentary here.

4 Demanding More

1 'Trade Union and Labour Relations (Consolidation) Act 1992', Part V, 244, legislation.gov.uk/ukpga/1992/52/part/V.

2 Labor Notes, 'How to Strike and Win', *Labor Notes*, 2019, labornotes. org.

3 Joe Burns, *Strike Back: Using the Militant Tactics of Labor's Past to Reignite Public Sector Unionism Today*, New York: IG Publishers, 2014.

4 Migration News, 'French Police Remove Immigrants from Church', *Migration News* 3: 9, 1996, migration.ucdavis.edu.

5 Marion Quintin, 'The CGT Campaign Supporting the 'Sans-Papiers', Cornell University, Summer, 2009, archive.ilr.cornell.edu.

6 Ibid.

7 David Harvey, *A Brief History of Neoliberalism*, Oxford: Oxford University Press, 2005.

8 William Finnegan, 'Leasing the Rain', *New Yorker*, 31 March 2002, newyorker.com.

9 Quoted in ibid.

10 Oscar Olivera, *¡Cochabamba!: Water War in Bolivia*, Cambridge, MA: South End Press, 2004, 25.

11 Ibid., 25.

12 Ibid., 28.

13 Finnegan, 'Leasing the Rain'.

14 Olivera, *¡Cochabamba!*, 31.

15 Ibid, 31.

16 Finnegan, Leasing the Rain'.

17 Olivera, *¡Cochabamba!*, 28.

18 Jeffrey R. Webber, 'The Rebellion in Bolivia', *Against the Current*, 116, 2005.

19 Oscar Olivera, 'The Voice of the People can Dilute Corporate Power', *The Guardian*, 19 July 2006, theguardian.com.

5 Fighting for Liberation

1 James Arrowsmith, 'British Airways' Heathrow Flights Grounded by Dispute at Gate Gourmet', *Eurofound*, 19 September 2005, eurofound. europa.eu.

2 Anti-Apartheid Movement Archives, 'Trade Unions Against Apartheid', 2021, aamarchives.org.

3 Kevin Maguire, 'Anti-War Train Drivers Refuse to Move Arms Freight', *The Guardian*, 9 January 2003, theguardian.com.

4 Martin Williams, 'Glasgow Council Faces Strike Action Over £500m Equal Pay Row', *The Herald*, 4 October 2021, heraldscotland.com.

5 Libby Brooks, 'Women Win 12-Year Equal Pay Battle with Glasgow City Council', *The Guardian*, 17 January 2019, theguardian.com.

6 ONS, 'Gender Pay Gap in the UK: 2021', Office for National Statistics, 2021, ons.gov.

7 ONS, 'Ethnicity Pay Gaps: 2019', Office for National Statistics, 2020, ons.gov.

8 Department of Labor, 'Earning Disparities by Sex', 2022, dol.gov.

9 Department of Labor, 'Earning Disparities by Race and Ethnicity', 2022, dol.gov.

10 Tech Workers Coalition, 'Issue 25: Google Walkout Ripples Across the Industry', 9 November 2018, techworkerscoalition.org.

11 Cecilia D'Anastasio, 'Riot Settles Lawsuit, Will Pay Every Female Employee Since 2014 With $10 Million Fund', *Kotaku*, 2 December 2019, kotaku.com.

12 Maeve Allsup, 'Activision Blizzard Sued Over "Frat Boy" Culture, Harassment', *Bloomberg Law*, 21 July 2021, news.bloomberglaw.com.

13 TUC, 'Still Just a Bit of Banter', Trades Union Congress, 2016, tuc.org.uk.

6 Work

1 ONS, 'Labour Costs and Labour Income, UK: 2021', Office for National Statistics, 2021, ons.gov.

2 James Manyika et al., 'A New Look at the Declining Labor Share of Income in the United States', McKinsey Global Institute, 2019 mckinsey.com.

3 Marx, *Capital: A Critique of Political Economy, Volume 1*, London: Penguin Books, [1867] 1977, 899.

4 Karl Marx, *Capital*, 125.

5 Ibid., 272.

6 For a longer discussion of this see Marx, *Capital*, 283.

7 Management

1 E.P. Thompson, *The Making of the English Working Class*, London: Penguin, 1991, 213.

2 Angela Davis, *Women, Race & Class*, London: Penguin, [1981] 2019.

3 Noel Ignatiev, *How the Irish Became White*, Abingdon: Routledge, 1995.

4 Arun Kundani, *The Muslims are Coming! Islamophobia, Extremism, and the Domestic War on Terror*, London: Verso, 2014.

5 Jamie Woodcock, *Working the Phones: Control and Resistance in Call*

Centres, London: Pluto, 2017.

6 Friedrich Engels, *The Origin of the Family, Private Property and the State*, London: Penguin, [1884] 2010.

7 Mariarosa Dalla Costa and Selma James, *The Power of Women and the Subversion of the Community*, Bristol: Falling Wall Press, 1972.

8 David Graeber, *Bullshit Jobs*, London: Simon & Schuster, 2019, 31.

9 Erik Olin Wright, *Class Structure and Income Determination*, London: Academic Press, 1979, 39.

10 Richard Edwards, *Contested Terrain: The Transformation of the Workplace in the Twentieth Century*, New York: Basic Books, 1979, 12.

11 Frederick W. Taylor, *The Principles of Scientific Management*, New York: Norton, 1967.

12 Harry Braverman, *Labor and Monopoly Capitalism: The Degradation of Work in the Twentieth Century*, London: Monthly Review, 1999, 82, 60.

13 UTAW, 'What is Employee Surveillance', United Tech and Allied Workers, 2021, utaw.tech.

8 Conflict

1 Carter L. Goodrich, *Frontier of Control: Study in British Workshop Politics*, London: Pluto, 1975.

2 CIPD, 'Managing Conflict in the Modern Workplace', Chartered Institute of Personnel and Development, January 2020, cipd.co.uk.

3 Deborah Hann and David Nash, 'Disputes and Their Management in the Workplace: A Survey of British Employers', ACAS, 30 April 2020, acas.org.uk.

4 Richard Saundry and Peter Urwin, 'Estimating the Costs of Workplace Conflict', ACAS, 11 May 2021, acas.org.uk.

5 David Cooper and Teresa Kroeger, 'Employers Steal Billions from Workers' Paychecks Each Year', Economic Policy Institute, 10 May 2017, www.epi.org.

6 Brady Meixell and Ross Eisenbrey, 'An Epidemic of Wage Theft is Costing Workers Hundreds of Millions of Dollars a Year', Economic Policy Institute, 11 September 2014, www.epi.org.

7 HM Revenue & Customs, 'HMRC Reveals Absurd Excuses for Not Paying National Minimum Wage', 17 August 2021, gov.uk.

8 Living Wage Foundation, 2021, livingwage.org.uk.

9 US Department of Labor, 2022, dol.gov/general/topic/wages/minimumwage.

10 Ihna Mangundayao, Celine McNicholas, Margaret Poydock and Ali Sait, 'More Than $3 billion in Stolen Wages Recovered for Workers between 2017 and 2020', Economic Policy Institute, 2021, epi.org/publication/wage-theft-2021.

11 Ibid.

12 Marx, *Capital*, 352.

13 Nina Golgowski, 'Man Skipped Work For 6 Years And No One Noticed Until He Won An Award', *Huffington Post*, 16 February 2016, huffingtonpost.co.uk.

14 George Rawick, 'Working Class Self-Activity', *Radical America* 3: 2, 1969, 23–31.

15 William F. Edgerton, 'The Strikes in Ramses III's Twenty-ninth Year', *Journal of Near Eastern Studies* 10: 3, 1951, 137–45.

16 Greg Grandin, *The Empire of Necessity*, New York: Metropolitan Books, 2014, 146.

17 Richard Hyman, *Strikes*, Basingstoke: Macmillan, 1989, 17.

18 Geoffrey Hughes, *An Encyclopedia of Swearing*, London: Routledge, 2015.

19 UCU, 'Reclaim our Time: ASOS Campaign', 2021, ucu.org.uk/reclaim-our-time.

20 *RTBU Express*, 'Sydney Bus Drivers Let Commuters Ride Free in Protest against Privatisation', 1 June 2017, rtbuexpress.com.au.

21 Huffington Post Canada, 'Cathay Pacific Smile Strike', *Huffington Post*, 13 December 2012, huffpost.com.

22 Root & Branch, *Root & Branch: The Rise of the Workers' Movement*, Greenwich, CT: Fawcett Publications, 1975, 209.

23 Quoted in Mike Davis, 'The Stopwatch and the Wooden Shoe', *Radical America* 9: 1, 1975.

24 Ibid.

25 Beyond Europe, 'Hands of VIO.ME', *Beyond Europe*, 30 March 2020. beyondeurope.net.

26 Jamie Woodcock, 'Deliveroo and UberEATS: Organizing in the Gig Economy in the UK', Global Disconnections, 2016, concessioniprecarie.org.

9 Trade Unionism

1 Tolpuddle Martyrs, tolpuddlemartyrs.org.uk.

2 David Corbin, *Gun Thugs, Rednecks, and Radicals: A Documentary History of the West Virginia Mine Wars*, Oakland: PM Press, 2011.

3 Chris Bell, 'Delta Airline Staff Told "Don't Unionise, Buy Video Games" ', *BBC*, 10 May 2019, bbc.co.uk.

4 Jay Peters, 'Whole Foods is Reportedly Using a Heat Map to Track Stores at Risk of Unionization', *The Verge*, 20 April 2020, theverge.com.

5 Perceptyx, 'Influence the Future with Predictive Analytics in HR', 2019, blog.perceptyx.com.

6 BCG, 'About Us', Bargaining for the Common Good, 2021, bargainingforthecommongood.org.

7 CLB, 'Workers' Right and Labour Relations in China', *China Labour Bulletin*, 30 June 2020, clb.org.hk.

8 Kim Moody, *An Injury to All: The Decline of American Unionism*, London: Verso, 1988, 15.

9 Jane McAlevey, *No Shortcuts: Organizing for Power in the New Gilded Age*, Oxford: Oxford University Press, 2016.

10 Melanie Simms and Jane Holgate, 'Organizing for What?', *Work, Employment and Society* 24: 1, 2010, 157–68.

11 Karl Marx, *Value, Price and Profit*, New York: International, [1898] 1969.

12 Friedrich Engels, *The Conditions of the Working Class in England*, Oxford: Oxford University Press, [1845] 2009, 232.

13 Hal Draper, 'Marxism and Trade Unions', 1970, marxists.org.

14 Ray, 'What is the Rank-and-File Strategy?', *Notes from Below*, 3 November 2021, notesfrombelow.org.

15 Alice Lynd and Staughton Lynd, *Rank & File: Personal Histories by Working-Class Organizers*, Chicago: Haymarket, 2011.

16 Aaron Brenner, Robert Brenner and Cal Winslow, *Rebel Rank and File: Labor Militancy and Revolt from Below During the Long 1970s*, London: Verso, 2010.

17 Draper, 'Marxism and Trade Unions'.

18 Labor Notes, see labornotes.org.

19 Strike Map, see strikemap.co.uk.

10 Workers' Inquiries

1 For a longer discussion of this, see Clark McAllister, *Karl Marx's Workers' Inquiry: International History, Reception, and Responses*, London: Notes from Below, 2022.

2 Karl Marx, 'A Workers' Inquiry', *La Revue Socialiste*, 20 April 1880. marxists.org.

3 Jamie Woodcock, 'The Workers' Inquiry from Trotskyism to Operaismo: A Political Methodology for Investigating the Workplace', *Ephemera* 14: 3, 2014, 493–513.

4 Notes from Below, 'Introduction: Why Worker Writing Matters', 7 October 2020, notesfrombelow.org.

5 Notes from Below, 'From the Workplace', 7 October 2020, notesfrombelow.org.

6 Notes from Below, 'The Workers' Inquiry and Social Composition', 29 January 2018, notesfrombelow.org.

7 Karl Marx, *A Contribution to the Critique of Political Economy*, Moscow: Progress Publishers, 1977.

8 Ed Emery, 'No Politics Without Inquiry!', *Common Sense* 18, 1995.

11 Action

1 Hyman, *Strikes*.
2 Rosa Luxemburg, *Reform or Revolution and the Mass Strike*, Chicago: Haymarket, [1899/1906] 2007.
3 James Brooks, *American Syndicalism: The IWW*, New York: Macmillan, 1913, 135.
4 *The Guardian*, 'Fight for Your Rights: The Trade Union for Outsourced Workers', *YouTube*, 12 August 2020, youtube.com/watch?v=asUEj0uCpjE.

12 The Rank and File

1 Draper, 'Marxism and Trade Unions'.
2 Will Gallacher, 'Clyde Workers' Committee: To All Clyde Workers', 1915, marxists.org.
3 Sally Hunt, 'A Little Less Conversation', *The Guardian*, 12 April 2005, theguardian.com.
4 Online versions of the bulletin can be found on notesfrombelow.org and we made a podcast about the process: notesfrombelow.org/article/university-worker-podcast.
5 Jamie Woodcock and Sai Englert, 'Looking Back in Anger: The UCU Strikes', *Notes from Below*, 30 August 2018, notesfrombelow.org.

13 Democracy

1 Hal Draper, 'The Two Souls of Socialism', *New Politics* 5: 1, 1966, marxists.org.

14 The Bigger Horizon

1 Kristin Ross, *Communal Luxury: The Political Imaginary of the Paris Commune*, London: Verso, 2015, 1.
2 Karl Marx, 'The Civil War in France', 1871, marxists.org.
3 Der Sozialdemokrat, 'Gedenktage des Proletariats: Die blutige Maiwoche', Der Sozialdemokrat, 21, 1881, 1.
4 Karl Marx and Frederick Engels, 'Preface to the 1872 German Edition of the Communist Manifesto', 1872, marxists.org.

5　C.L.R. James, Raya Dunayevskaya and Grace Lee Boggs, *State Capitalism and World Revolution*, Oakland, CA: PM Press, [1950] 2013; Tony Cliff, *State Capitalism in Russia*, London: Bookmarks, [1955] 1974.
6　Felix Morrow, *Revolution and Counter-revolution in Spain*, London: Pathfinder, 1974.
7　Chris Harman, *The Fire Last Time: 1968 and After*, London: Bookmarks, 1998.
8　Colin Barker, *Revolutionary Rehearsals*, Chicago: Haymarket, 2002.
9　Michael Knapp, Anja Flach and Ercan Ayboga, *Revolution in Rojava*, London: Pluto, 2016.
10　V.I. Lenin, 'The Discussion on Self-Determination Summed up', *Lenin Collected Works*, 22, 1916, marxists.org.
11　See, for example, the Working Class History podcast, workingclasshistory.com.
12　David Graeber, *The Utopia of Rules: On Technology, Stupidity, and the Secret Joys of Bureaucracy*, London: Melville House, 2015, 89.

Conclusion: Putting Troublemaking into Practice

1　Hal Draper, 'Marxism and Trade Unions', 1970, marxists.org.
2　C.L.R. James, 'Every Cook Can Govern', *Correspondence* 2: 12, 1956.
3　Martin Glaberman, 'Workers Have to Deal with Their Own Reality and That Transforms Them', 1997, marxists.org.
4　Karl Marx, 'Preface to the 1888 English Edition of the Communist Manifesto', (1888) marxists.org.
5　Rosa Luxemburg, *Reform or Revolution and the Mass Strike*, Chicago: Haymarket, [1899/1906] 2007.
6　Sai Englert, 'Notes on Organisation', *Notes from Below*, 22 June 2020, notesfrombelow.org.
7　Glaberman, 'Workers Have to Deal'.
8　Maurice Brinton, 'As We See It', *Solidarity* 4: 6, 1967.
9　V.I. Lenin, 'The Collapse of the Second International', *Collected Works, Volume 21: August 1914–December 1915*, Moscow: Progress Publishers, 1964, 213–14.